THE CYCLE OF
VICTORIOUS LIVING:

*Commit, trust, delight,
and rest in Jesus Christ*

By T. Scott Daniels
with Earl and Hazel Lee

BEACON HILL PRESS
OF KANSAS CITY

ISBN 978-0-8341-2610-7

Printed in the
United States of America

Cover Design: J.R. Caines
Interior Design: Sharon Page

Library of Congress Cataloging-in-Publication Data

Lee, Earl G.
   The cycle of victorious living : commit, trust, delight, and rest in Jesus
Christ / T. Scott Daniels and Earl G. Lee.
       p. cm.
   "1971 original version of The cycle of victorious living, by Earl G. Lee"—
P.
   ISBN 978-0-8341-2610-7 (pbk.)
   1. Christian life—Nazarene authors. 2. Bible. O.T. Psalms XXXVII—
Devotional use. 3. Peace of mind—Religious aspects—Christianity.
I. Daniels, T. Scott, 1966- II. Title.
   BV4501.1.L424 2012
   248.4'8799—dc23

                                                                2011048736

10 9 8 7 6 5 4

To the Lees, the Tippitts, and the people of PazNaz, who have allowed me to share their victorious legacy.

CONTENTS

ACKNOWLEDGMENTS

My sincere thanks to

—Bonnie Perry and Beacon Hill Press for encouraging this unique collaboration.

—Grant Lee and Gayle Lee Tippitt for giving not only their permission but also their blessing to adding to their father's significant legacy.

—the wonderful people of Pasadena First Nazarene (PazNaz) for loving and living the victorious cycle so much that they were willing not only to sit through it but also to embrace it again

—my amazing wife, Debbie, and my four great kids— Caleb, Noah, Jonah, and Sophie—for loving me and walking the way of God with me.

Do not fret because of the wicked; do not be envious of wrongdoers,

for they will soon fade like the grass, and wither like the green herb.

*Trust in the L*ORD*, and do good; so you will live in the land, and enjoy security.*

*Take delight in the L*ORD*, and he will give you the desires of your heart.*

*Commit your way to the L*ORD*; trust in him, and he will act.*

He will make your vindication shine like the light, and the justice of your cause like the noonday.

*Be still before the L*ORD*, and wait patiently for him; do not fret over those who prosper in their way, over those who carry out evil devices.*

Refrain from anger, and forsake wrath.

Do not fret—it leads only to evil.

—Psalm 37:1-8

PREFACE

Until the Lord returns or Pasadena First Church of the Nazarene closes its doors, every pastor at "PazNaz" will likely walk in the shadow of Dr. Earl Lee. Pastor Lee retired from full-time ministry in 1984 and went to be with the Lord in 1998, but his visionary leadership, insightful teaching, and joy for living helped countless people enter into a dynamic and eternal relationship with the Heavenly Father. It has been an honor for me to walk in his shadow for the last five years and carry on the legacy he established in Pasadena.

Pastor Lee's beloved sermon series *The Cycle of Victorious Living* was first published in 1971 and has sold over 100,000 copies and has been translated into six languages. In honor of the anniversary of the writing of *The Cycle*, I recently "recycled" this great series on Psalm 37 for a new generation of believers at PazNaz. Although many members at the church can still quote with ease the four main parts of "the cycle"—commit, trust, delight, rest—there were far more who needed to hear for the first time the beautiful insight the Lord gave to Pastor Lee from His Word during a time of uncertainty, fear, and worry. My pastoral team helped me dig around through the archives and find recordings of Dr. Lee preaching and teaching the series for which he was so well known, so with a little editing here and there, it was a privilege to preach *The Cycle of Victorious Living* with Dr. Lee. His voice would begin and end each message while I tried to fill in some thoughts in between. This newest edition of Earl's original work is the result of that series. Working through and expanding on his original material was a renewed blessing for me, and I hope it will be for you as well.

In the chapters that follow you will find my thoughts and reflections on Psalm 37 and *The Cycle of Victorious Living*, and you will also find my attempt to reframe *The Cycle* into a twenty-first-century context. Much like the sermon series we preached together, in each chapter I let Dr. Lee have the first and last word. It is often said by theologians that all of theology is a footnote to Augustine. I'm sure my contributions will in many ways be a footnote to Earl's inspired original work. For that reason, in addition to my chapters, you will find Dr. Lee's original text—in its entirety—at the end of the book.

Although we were born half a century apart and our tenures at Pasadena First are separated by three decades, I thought Pastor Lee and I made a pretty good preaching team. It is my hope that the combination of our thoughts and eras will invite those of you who are revisiting *The Cycle* or reading it for the very first time to hear God's voice inviting you into the victorious and gracious life He has for you.

one

FRET NOT
THERE AIN'T NO REST
FOR THE WICKED

Oswald Chambers says, "All our fret and worry is caused by calculating without God." It destroys victorious living as surely as insects and other pests destroy leaves. . . . Fret is the snail under the leaf, and in order to have lives of fragrance and beauty, these snails of fret must go. And God has a specially prepared way for their exit. It is found in the cycle of victorious living.
—*Earl Lee*

My teenage sons work hard to try to keep me young and hip. Not long ago they introduced me to a band named Cage the Elephant. The Kentucky rock band's first hit song, entitled "Ain't No Rest for the Wicked," is pretty catchy, but I have become fascinated mainly by its message. The song contains three verses that serve as a kind of testimonial of lament. The singer tells the story of three separate and somewhat broken encounters. In the first verse he stumbles across a prostitute who propositions him. He declines her offer, but he wants to know why she has chosen to live her life working the streets. The second verse is about the singer coming face to face with a mugger who takes all his money, but before he goes on his way, the singer asks him why he wants to live this kind of life. The last verse is about a preacher who is arrested for taking all the "righteous dollar bills" from his congregation. The singer recognizes this as a despicable act but one he can identify with nonetheless.

In each situation the singer asks the person why he or she has chosen this kind of life. In each case the chorus of the song is the reply. The person has chosen to sell himself or herself, steal from the vulnerable, or forfeit his or her soul for money—because there is no rest for the wicked until our eyes close for good: money doesn't grow on trees; there are mouths to feed; and nothing is free.

I'm not sure if the members of Cage the Elephant have ever read Psalm 37, but nevertheless, I think they may have given us a very clear picture of part of its message. According to the psalmist, all people have two paths to choose from: life or death, light or dark, Yahweh (the Lord) or idols, the narrow road that leads to life or the broad road that leads to destruction. According to the Scripture, there is no third option. One has a choice between the way of the Lord or the way of the wicked.

The way of the Lord is described in Psalm 37 with words like *trust, good, security, delight, commitment, vindication, justice, stillness,* and *patience*. In contrast, the way of the wicked is described using words such as *envy, evil, schemes, devices, anger, wrath, plots, violence,* and *insecurity*.

Jesus picks up on this identical theme in the Sermon on the Mount. In Matthew 6 He connects "the way of the wicked" described in Psalm 37 with the way of the Gentiles. Jesus proclaims,

No one can serve two masters; for a slave will either hate the one and love the other, or be devoted to the one and despise the other. You cannot serve God and wealth.

Therefore I tell you, do not worry about your life, what you will eat or what you will drink, or about your body, what you will wear. Is not life more than food, and the body more than clothing? Look at the birds of the air; they neither sow nor reap nor gather into barns, and yet your heavenly Father feeds them. Are you not of more value than they? And can any of you by worrying add a single hour to your span of life? And why do you worry about clothing? Consider the lilies of the field, how they grow; they neither toil nor spin, yet I tell you, even Solomon in all his glory was not clothed like one of these. But if God so clothes the grass of the field, which is alive today and tomorrow is thrown into the oven, will he not much more clothe you—you of little faith? Therefore do not worry, saying "What will we eat?" or "What will we drink?" or "What will we wear?" For it is the Gentiles who strive for all these things; and indeed your heavenly Father knows that you need all these things.

But strive first for the kingdom of God and his righteousness, and all these things will be given to you as well.

So do not worry about tomorrow, for tomorrow will bring worries of its own. Today's trouble is enough for today *(Matthew 6:24-34).*

Like the psalmist, Jesus proclaims that there are only two options from which to choose. A person can choose to serve God *or* serve wealth. No one can serve both. According to Jesus, the lifestyles exhibited by the Gentiles or pagans reveal that they have already made their choice. They have chosen to serve the god described in the sermon as wealth or "mammon." To serve wealth or mammon is to live a life dedicated almost exclusively to the pursuit of money, food, clothing, and extravagant homes. The problem with choosing this life is that it looks like such an appealing road to take. Unfortunately, when a person chooses this way of life, instead of reaping blessings, he or she reaps curses. Sadly, what appears to be the road to life is actually the road to death. And most interestingly, in both Psalm 37 and Matthew 6, what appears to be the way of security is actually the way of instability and worry.

In both passages of Scripture, for both the psalmist and Jesus, the wrong road in life—the way of the wicked or the way of the Gentiles—is marked by the same torment: worry or fret. Significantly, the command in both passages of Scripture is the same: do not fret and do not worry. Fret is not just the on-ramp to the way of the wicked; it is the quality that defines the life devoted to serving the god of wealth. The cycle of non-victorious living, if you will, is the life people live worrying about what they will eat, fretting about what they will wear, or obsessing about where they will live.

The way of the wicked for the psalmist, or the way of the Gentiles for Jesus, is not just lived by individuals; it is embodied in economic systems, political structures, and in cultures. The way of the wicked is embodied in what can be referred to as "empires." "Empire" is a good word to describe the various powers and cultural systems that the people of God confront throughout the Bible. The empires of the Scripture go by names such as Egypt, Canaan, Assyria,

Babylon, and Rome. In each of these cases, Israel—as God's people or nation—has to learn to live in ways that are a holy contrast to the various ways of these empires. No matter what era or time period is addressed in the Scripture, the challenge seems to be the same: how do the people of God live as His unique people in the midst of principalities and powers—empires—that try to lure them and conform them to their hurried and worried way of life?

But why, if the way of the wicked leads to death, do so many people follow after it? What makes the way of worry so appealing? The way of the wicked, the way of the Gentiles, or what I am referring to as the way of the empire, is formed and sustained through various myths people tell themselves about themselves. Following are some of the primary myths of the empire that are told every day.

The first myth that dominates the cultures and empires all around us is **the myth of value**. One of the most significant convictions of "empire" is that life is found in what we eat, what we wear, and where we live. At some level all human beings must consume or use food, clothing, and shelter. But the myth of value teaches us the importance of conspicuous consumption. Conspicuous consumption means that what I eat, what I wear, and where I live add value to me as a person. Since that is the case, then I want to eat expensive food, wear fashionable clothing with the right labels, and live in a prestigious neighborhood—because if other people see me driving an expensive car or wearing expensive brand names, that will mean that I am a person of high value. But this kind of life makes sense only if others see it, so I must be as conspicuous as possible in my consumption so that others will recognize how valuable I am. This is why hood ornaments matter on a car and why clothing manufacturers put their labels on the outside of their clothes. Thus, the way of the wicked is almost always associated with symbols of status.

Another important myth of empire is **the myth of consumptive emptiness**. This myth says that as a person my primary problem is that I am empty and need to be filled. It is true that God gave us certain appetites—such as the desire for food and sexual intimacy—so we would survive as individuals and as cultures. But if we become shaped by the myth of consumption and focus our lives on our desires, we end up feeding appetites that can never be fully satisfied.

Have you ever noticed how almost every television commercial operates as if it's a parable? At the beginning of an advertisement the viewer is shown a glimpse of despair, emptiness, and futility. I remember an ad that was on when I was young that celebrated a new detergent that would remove any "ring around the collar." The ad would begin with a couple in a restaurant where the waitress noticed that the man had ring around the collar. Soon everyone eating around them recognized the horror of the man's dirty collar as well. He was caught in the pit of ring-around-the-collar despair—until salvation was discovered halfway through the ad in the form of a new detergent that took care of ring around the collar. The ad ended with the couple back in the same restaurant, only this time the waitress and everyone present smiled broadly as they recognized that the man no longer bore the burden of ring around the collar. Salvation had been found on the right grocery store aisle.

Each time the product is different—traveler's checks, medications, sneakers, cars, or mops—but the message is the same: you are currently empty and in despair. But if you buy this product, you will find the bliss and happiness you are currently missing. You are an empty person needing to be filled with one more purchase or one more product. The only problem is that the system can be sustained only if no one ever finds a place of satisfaction. The carrot of fulfillment must always be just out of reach for the myth of consumptive emptiness to continue.

Another significant myth for the empire is **the myth of scarcity**. One of the primary stories that shapes cultures and nations is the story that there aren't enough resources for all people to share and be sustained. Therefore, when you receive the significant resources of life, you must gather them, hoard them, and defend them. If you don't, those who are without enough resources will take them away from you. This dangerous myth fuels humankind's inclination to covet, and it inevitably leads to violence.

Think of the contrast in the Old Testament that God forms between Egypt and Israel. Egypt, fearful that there would never be enough, built storehouses to hoard all its wealth so that its power could never be taken away. In contrast, when God delivers Israel into the wilderness, He teaches them to depend upon Him for daily bread (manna) and to live in ways that allow for trust to take root. It is apparently one kind of miracle for God to get Israel out of Egypt; it is another miracle altogether to get Egypt out of Israel!

A final myth that shapes the life of the wicked or the Gentiles is **the myth of control**. Every principality or power—or empire—acquires strength and allegiance by convincing people that it is powerful, mighty, eternal, and in control. I believe this is the reason God had Moses bring the ten plagues on Pharaoh and on Egypt. Each plague deconstructed the myth of control Pharaoh had established with his people. Pharaoh was convinced that he was in control, but more importantly, he needed *his people* to be convinced that he was in control. God sent ten powerful reminders to Pharaoh that his control was nothing more than a myth.

These last few years of economic recession have been a challenge for many, many people in America and around the world. I am convinced that one way God works and redeems through economic downturns is to use them as reminders for all of us that even the economic security of a modern political superpower is essentially a myth. The Scripture frequently reminds the people of God that "the wicked will fade like grass," because we need to be reminded daily that God and not the principalities and powers are in charge.

But there is good news. There is another path to walk. There is another way to live. It is the *victorious* way of living. To live victoriously does not mean that in a highly competitive world we will always "win" in the same terms that the world sees winning. It is not a life free from suffering. It is not a life where our health is always good and our children always obey us. It is not a life where the bills always get paid with plenty of money to spare. The way of victorious living is the way of peace. It is the way of security in the midst of turmoil. It is the life built on the Solid Rock that is able to stand in the midst of the storms and turbulence of life.

In contrast to the tumultuous, fret-filled life of the wicked, the way of God's people is the way of *shalom*—the Hebrew word for peace—marked in particular by the practice of the Sabbath. *Shalom*—or peace—is mentioned two hundred forty-seven times in the Bible, and it is usually referenced in connection to the way of God's kingdom or the state of God's people. Shalom is the way of the original life for Adam and Eve (and all of creation) in the Garden of Eden. For Jesus in the Sermon on the Mount, shalom is the way of the birds, the lilies, and even the grass of the fields. Shalom is the way our loving Heavenly Father wants His children to live.

The Sabbath is mentioned one hundred-forty-four times in Scripture. To honor or keep God's Sabbath intentions is not simply the complete avoidance of work for one day a week so we can burn ourselves out the other six days. Sabbath is rather that practice that keeps our work in proper perspective. For the people of God, the goal of work is not more work. As we discover in the creation story of Genesis 1, the pinnacle of God's creative work is the Sabbath. We rest on the seventh day because God concluded His act of creation with a Sabbath or shalom for all of creation. The high point of God's work is the opportunity to rest and celebrate with Him.

As we will discover moving forward together, Psalm 37 offers four principles for finding the life of shalom with God. But before we can live into those four principles, we must first put away fret. We must move from worrying about what we will eat, what we will wear, or where we will live to a Sabbath trust and celebration in God.

A Sabbath mentality certainly does not come easily for people caught in the cycle of consumption and security offered by the empire. It is very easy for each of us to get caught up in the patterns of consumerism and accumulation that mark the way of the wicked. But this is the way of destruction. It is the way of fret and worry.

Remember: there ain't no rest for the wicked! But a "Sabbath rest still remains for the people of God; for those who enter God's rest also cease from their labours as God did from his. Let us therefore make every effort to enter that rest, so that no one may fall through such disobedience as theirs" (Hebrews 4:9-11).

I am not proposing an impossible way of life. I am not saying one will never fret. But I do maintain there is a cycle of victorious living, a working in and a working out of 1 Corinthians, chapter 13, whereby life ever has an upbeat. When we realize we are becoming victims of fret, that we are getting out of orbit, we ask forgiveness and get back into the cycle by once more committing our way unto the Lord. —*Earl Lee*

CHAPTER DISCUSSION QUESTIONS

Chapter 1: Fret Not:
There Ain't No Rest for the Wicked

1. How do God's people live in contrast to "principalities and powers" that try to conform us to a hurried and worried way of life?

_____

_____

_____

_____

_____

_____

2. Read and reflect on Matthew 6:24-34. How do Jesus' words challenge you?

_____

_____

_____

_____

_____

_____

3. Where do you see the "myth of value" around you? In what ways are you or have you been tempted by this myth?

_____

_____

_____

_____

_____

_____

4. "It is apparently one kind of miracle for God to get Israel out of Egypt; it is another miracle altogether to get Egypt out of Israel!" What is the author saying in this quote in regard to the "myth of scarcity?"

_____

_____

_____

_____

_____

_____

5. How is our world reminded on a regular basis that the control we have over our lives is limited?

_____

_____

_____

_____

_____

_____

6. How are Shalom and Sabbath in direct contrast with the life of fret?

_____

_____

_____

_____

_____

_____

two

COMMIT
AND KEEP ON COMMITTING

> **Commitment is something other than a sentimental decision that may change one's life for a few emotion-filled days. It is a valid act of the will changing one's whole way of life. It is one's entrance into the cycle of victorious living.** *—Earl Lee*

I travel quite a bit, which makes me a frequent flyer. I am not afraid of being in an airplane. I am rational enough to know that air travel is by far the safest and most efficient way to get from one place to another. But even though I would not label myself a nervous flyer, there is a moment each time I'm on a plane that causes me to grip the arm rest a little tighter and my heart to skip a beat or two. It is that moment at takeoff when the plane reaches full speed on the runway and begins to leave the ground. It is the moment when the pilot has fully committed the plane—and therefore all of the passengers on board—to only one of two possibilities. In that moment the plane is going to rise into the air and fly the way it was designed to operate, or something very, very bad is going to happen. It is the point of no return.

Up until that moment of takeoff I had many chances to turn back. I could have decided to stay home and not travel. Even once I made it to the airport I could have decided not to give the attendant my ticket and just stay in an overpriced airport restaurant and eat. Even once the plane began pulling away from the gate I could get up and cause enough commotion that an air marshal is called and I'm placed under arrest. But once the plane begins to lift off, I'm committed. From that moment on, the plane's destiny and my own future are inseparably fused together.

I have a friend who likes to skydive—something I have never been tempted in the least to do. She tells me that the great moment for a skydiver is when the diver steps out of the plane and the commitment to jump has been made. From that point on there is no option but to fall from the sky and hope the parachute works the way it is supposed to.

The psalmist lets us know that the exit ramp out of the cycle of victorious living is fret. But what is the onramp into the life of shalom that God has for His people? It is commitment. It is to "commit your way to the LORD" (Psalm 37:5).

One of the breakthrough moments for Pastor Lee, as he studied Psalm 37, was reading the text in Marathi. "The true meaning of the word *commit* came to me as I was reading this passage in Marathi, our 'stepmother' tongue of India. If I were to make a free translation of the Marathi, it says, 'Turn what you are and what you have over to God— palms down!'" Commitment is to take whatever we are carrying in our hands—including our worries and concerns— and giving them to God with hands open and palms down.

The apostle Paul has a great deal to say about commitment in his letter to the Roman church. In Romans 6 he reminds the Roman believers about the significance of their baptism. "What then are we to say? Should we continue in sin in order that grace may abound? By no means! How can we who died to sin go on living in it? Do you not know that all of us who have been baptized into Christ Jesus were baptized into his death? Therefore we have been . . . raised from the dead by the glory of the Father, so we too might walk in newness of life" (Romans 6:1-4 NRSV).

The sacrament of baptism finds its roots in the Exodus story. In the tenth plague—the death angel—God called the Israelites to break their identification with Pharaoh and place their identity in the lamb at the center of the Passover table by marking the doorposts of their homes with its blood. Those who identified their lives in this way with the lamb were spared the judgment of God and were released from slavery. But while the Hebrew people were up against the banks of the Red Sea, Pharaoh hardened his heart, changed his mind, and called for his chariots and soldiers to go and get his slaves back.

Moses raised his staff, and the waters parted. When the people entered the water, they still belonged to Pharaoh. When they came out of the water, they were truly free. They were no longer the slaves of the Egyptian king; they were children of the Creator. They went into the sea with a broken identity; they came out of the sea as new creations.

This is the story Paul carries into his words about baptism. In baptism the believer identifies with the death and resurrection of Christ. Going into the water is like dying to the old self. Coming out of the water testifies to being resurrected to the new self. Like the Israelites, the believer enters the water reminded of his or her former life as a slave to sin and self. But also like the Israelites, when the believer comes out of the water, he or she emerges reminded of being transformed as God's redeemed child: God's new creation.

That should be the end of the story, shouldn't it? The old self has been put to death, the new has taken its place. Unfortunately, all of us who have been baptized in Christ know that new life isn't easy. As the great reformer Martin Luther once quipped, "In baptism the old Adam is drowned. But the old man is a very good swimmer."

Paul recognizes this problem for the Roman believers. After reminding them of their baptism in Romans 6:1-4, in verses 5-11 he reminds them that the resurrection of Christ means that death no longer has dominion over him. Likewise, believers must consider themselves "dead to sin and alive to God in Christ Jesus" (6:11). How then do believers live as though they are dead to sin, especially when Adam is such a good swimmer? Here are Paul's instructions:

Therefore do not let sin exercise dominion in your mortal bodies, to make you obey their passions. No longer present your members to sin as instruments of wickedness, but present yourselves to God as those who have been brought from death to life, and present your members to God as instruments of righteousness. For sin will have no dominion over you, since you are not under law but under grace *(Romans 6:12-14)*.

The word that is translated in the passage above as "present" is in a Greek form that insinuates not just a one-time presentation of the members of our body to God but as a continuous presentation. Thus, the text could read, "No longer present and keep on presenting your members to sin, but present and keep on presenting your members to God."

Entering into the cycle of victorious living is not just a one-time commitment. Entering and staying in the way of God's shalom requires us to commit and keep on committing our way—hands down—to the Lord.

Imagine that you were renting a house from an oppressive landlord who, like a bully, not only required you to pay rent that was well above fair market value but also required you to do things that no landlord has a right to ask. This terrible landlord is always threatening you with eviction, legal action, or even bodily harm if you do not give in to his demands. But one day you find another place to live. Your new landlord pays off your previous debts and invites you to live in a place of peace where the requirements of life are not oppressive but a blessing.

However, the old landlord keeps showing up at your door angrily insisting that you keep paying him and meeting his demands. Because of your previous patterns of obedience, you may be tempted to give in to his ultimatums. But you are not under his control anymore. He is not your landlord. You no longer owe him any rent. Whatever debts kept you living under fear to him have been paid in full.

Can you imagine if a new Pharaoh had shown up in the Promised Land and demanded that the Israelites come back and be his slaves? The people may have shaken with fear at first to see an Egyptian king and to hear the familiar threats. But then they would be reminded that they were living in a new land—a land where Pharaoh had no claim. They cannot give their bodies back over to Pharaoh's work. They have committed themselves—hands down—to the rule of Yahweh.

This is the way of commitment. When the fret, like an angry landlord who marks the way of the wicked, shows up at the door, the believers are to commit and keep on committing their way to the Lord. We cannot hold onto that fret; but hands down, commit our way to Him. This is the only way into the pattern of God's holy life.

It is interesting to read what Paul believes is the end of this "commit and keep on committing" kind of life. "The advantage you get," writes Paul, "is sanctification. The end is eternal life" (Romans 6:22). Sanctification is the state that we are in when all of life has been set aside and committed to God for His purposes. It is the life in which we have made God our pilot and our lives are now completely bound to His purposes. Like a trusting skydiver, we have stepped out of the plane of our old life with Him and our destinies are now one hundred percent in His hands. The life of commitment, holding nothing back, places all of life under the caring, compassionate reign of God.

The end of the way of fret is death, but the end of commitment is eternal life. In the Scripture, eternal life is not just the assurance that believers will live after death. Eternal life is also the quality of life that can be described only as abundant life in the present. It may seem counterintuitive to think of the life of freedom as the life of commitment. But that is the secret to the victorious life of shalom. The benefit of the hands-down, fret-free life is a life filled with God's presence and abundantly held in his peace.

True commitment means we wash our hands of ourselves and give to Him our all—totally, not on condition. When conditions are attached, our palms are held

upward; but deep commitment means our palms are down. It is the only way to enter the cycle of victorious living. It demands faith in the character of our God and not in the circumstances we see or understand . . . We face new situations constantly, and over and over new problems are fed into the cycle. But the process, once learned, becomes a glorious way of life. *—Earl Lee*

CHAPTER DISCUSSION QUESTIONS

Chapter 2: Commit: And Keep on Committing

1. Read and reflect on Romans 6:12-14. How do we commit and keep on committing our ways to the Lord? What disciplines and patterns must we incorporate into our lives to help us succeed in the victorious way of living?

_____

_____

_____

_____

2. In your observation, what do people fear committing to the most? Why?

_____

_____

_____

_____

3. What is the significance of giving over our worries, concerns, and baggage to God with our hands open and palms down?

_____

_____

_____

_____

4. What is the relationship between commitment and faith?

_____

_____

_____

_____

three

TRUST
LEAPERS AND CALCULATORS

> "Pastor, I have really committed everything, including myself, to the Lord. Now what do I do?"
>
> "There is only one thing to do: lean hard! You have changed from independence to dependence. You don't just lean; you lean on Someone well able to carry your weight, the One who created the heavens and the earth and who never fails."   *—Earl Lee*

The way out of the cycle of victorious living is fret. The way into the cycle is to commit our way—hands down—to the Lord. The second step for continuing to walk in God's victorious way of peace is to trust in Him. "Trust in the LORD, and do good. . . . Trust in him, and he will act" (Psalm 37:3, 5).

The ability to trust, by faith, in the Lord is ultimately a gift of God's Spirit. But I am convinced that some people by nature receive and respond to that gift of trust and faith more naturally than others. I think people tend to either be leapers or calculators.

Leapers are people who seem to embrace the challenges of faith with little effort. They are naturally born risk-takers who are often able to translate that boldness into their journey with God. Calculators, on the other hand, are people who are by nature analytical. Whenever an opportunity emerges that may require a leap of faith, calculators immediately start analyzing the risks and the benefits. They start doing the math and calculating the odds. Leapers usually carry journals in their backpacks so they can write down all the amazing things God has done for them today. Calculators tend to carry yellow legal pads in case they have to make a decision during the day that might require them to draw a line down the middle of the page and start calculating out the pluses and the minuses of the situation.

My wife, Debbie, is a leaper; I am a calculator. We have four children. At this point it would appear that two of them are leapers, like their mother, and two of them are calculators, like their father.

Debbie and I believe that we have devised a method for discovering early in life whether your child is a leaper or a calculator. We believe you can tell if your son or daughter will by nature be open to leaps of faith or if they will by nature start analyzing the various options based on how they learn to swim when they are little.

Caleb, our oldest, is a calculator, which is somewhat unfortunate given that his biblical namesake was clearly a leaper. He is very much like me. He has a beautifully analytical mind. He learned to swim at a public pool near our home. Caleb's first calculation when we arrived at the pool was the number of rough-looking kids there that day. If there were too many potential bullies around, he immediately calculated the danger, and we were headed home before we even got wet. Once he was assured that we would be able to swim in peace, he would bend down so that he could look across the water to make sure there were no bugs or any other foreign objects floating in the water. Dead bees were especially problematic. If the surface of the water was clear and there was plenty of space to jump into the water without fear of landing on another swimmer, he would think about jumping in.

Our second son, Noah, much like his biblical namesake, is a leaper. As soon as we pulled up to the pool, Noah would throw open the van door and push his way through the crowd to get to the water as fast as he could while simultaneously yelling, "Cannonball!" as he ran.

Jonah is our third son, and he, like his biblical namebearer, is a calculator to an almost problematic degree. If Jonah calculated that it was a day worth leaving home, then he would join us at the pool. When we got to the pool, he would sit for twenty or thirty minutes—quite contentedly—with his feet dangling in the water. If that went well, he moved to the first step, where he would again spend twenty or thirty minutes. If all went according to plan there, he would eventually move down to the second step. Things, however, rarely went according to plan. On occasion Jonah even got his hair wet before it was time to go home.

Our only girl, Sophie, is a leaper. Her favorites on hot days at the pool were Popsicles. She would sit in a pool chair and eat three or four of them. But quite randomly she would decide that it was time to run and jump into the pool. Quite without warning—sometimes when I was at the completely opposite end of the pool—she yelled, "I'm jumping in, Dad!" She proceeded to leap into the water in complete trust that I would be able to swim or run fast enough to get to her before she drowned.

We'll see if our test holds true throughout their lives. But if it does, Noah and Sophie, like their mother, will tend to more easily respond to God's call to trust in Him, to leap into opportunities of childlike faith with Him. And if the pattern holds true, Caleb and Jonah, like their father, will carry around yellow legal pads and *desire* to trust the Lord—but will need to first do the math and calculate the challenges that lay ahead.

I don't think calculators offend God. In fact, I'm quite sure He created us with our analytical natures on purpose. Calculators often rise to important levels of leadership. Nearly every decision-making board I've served on is populated with calculators. When important decisions are being made, you want people around you who know how to analyze all the various options and calculate the risks involved. I think God has a big heart for calculators.

That is why I always feel bad for King Ahaz. If you open any handbook of the Bible and turn to the section on the good and bad kings of Israel and Judah, Ahaz inevitably makes the bad king list.

Here is the story of Ahaz. In 1 Samuel 8 the people of Israel demanded that a king be placed over them so they could be "like all the other nations." This was displeasing to both Samuel and the Lord, but after warning them that they would not like having a king, He permitted them to select one. It took only the reigns of three kings—Saul, David, and Solomon—for the people to realize that all the problems God had warned them about regarding kings were true. The nation divided into two, with ten tribes going north and forming the nation of Ephraim, or Israel, with their capital city of Samaria. The remaining two tribes—Judah and Benjamin—remained in the south and maintained the capital city of Jerusalem. In 722 B.C. the powerful nation of Assyria conquered and utterly destroyed Ephraim. Judah was able to hold off Assyria, but Babylon and King Nebuchadnezzar took them captive in 587 B.C.

Ahaz was the Judean ruler in Jerusalem from approximately 735-715 B.C., and his reign is described in 2 Kings 16, Isaiah 7-9, and 2 Chronicles 28. I want to focus on what we learn about him from the Book of Isaiah.

Christians tend to read Isaiah 7—9 during Advent season because of the ways Matthew interprets these texts in the light of the life of Jesus. When we read the prophets, however, I believe we need to read and interpret them on three levels. The first level is *original context*. What did this prophetic text mean in its original setting? The second level has to do with the way the *prophetic text* fits within the Messianic expectations and is therefore rightly associated with the life of Jesus Christ as the fulfillment of these prophetic hopes and expectations. But the third—and often neglected—level is the way these *prophetic hopes* still speak to the kind of leader God needs for His people today.

If we start at the first level—the original context—these chapters in Isaiah fall during the reign of Ahaz around 735 B.C. In that year Ahaz had a huge problem. King Rezin of Aram (Syria) and King Pekah of Ephraim (Israel) had created a coalition in an attempt to forge alliances among the small nations of the area in order to try to withstand the impending invasion from Assyria in the north. Pekah, the king of Ephraim, had tried to get Jotham, the father of Ahaz, to join the alliance against Assyria, but without success. Jotham refused to join, so Pekah, with the help of

Rezin of Aram, decided to send an army to Jerusalem to replace King Jotham with a puppet king who would agree to their demands to join the coalition. However, before their plan could succeed, Jotham died and left his son Ahaz to face the crisis.

In the midst of his fear, the prophet Isaiah arrives at the door. The great prophet gives Ahaz a message from the Lord. It is a simple message of trust: "Take heed, be quiet, do not fear, and do not let your heart be faint" (Isaiah 7:4). He even invites Ahaz to ask for a sign from the Lord as assurance of his promised deliverance. The sign could be as "deep as Sheol or high as heaven" (verse 11).

But Ahaz calculated. Here's what I believe he did: he heard the word of the Lord and then pulled out his yellow legal papyrus and started working out the math. He drew a line down the middle and wrote "Trust in the Lord" on one side and "Find another way out" on the other. He certainly calculated the size of his military forces compared to those of the alliance of Syria and Ephraim. He certainly considered his political future in the face of the will of the people. It had to be a fairly easy calculation. What the prophet was asking him to do simply did not add up.

Ahaz made his lack of faith sound spiritual—he did not want to "put God to the test"—but it was simply a decision not to trust. The inability to trust the Lord would lead Ahaz to make an unholy alliance with Tiglath-Pileser III, the king of Assyria. Like a scene out of a mafia movie, Ahaz melted down the gold from the temple and paid off Assyria for protection. The king of Assyria used the increased wealth and power to destroy Aram and Rezin (and all their people) and become the region's superpower.

I find this to be the way we most often respond when we fail to trust the Lord. We find differing roads around the way of trust. Those side routes tend to be forms of unholy alliances. A failure to trust inevitably leads not only back to the exit ramp of fret but often it leads us to places of compromise that, as they did for Ahaz, become the seeds for our ultimate destruction.

Despite his spiritual rhetoric, the prophet recognized the faithlessness of Ahaz for what it was and proclaimed,

> Hear then, O house of David! Is it too little for you to weary mortals, that you weary my God also? Therefore the Lord himself will give you a sign. Look, the young woman is with child and shall bear a son, and shall name him Immanuel. He shall eat curds and honey by the time he knows how to refuse the evil and choose the good. For before the child knows how to refuse the evil and choose the good, the land before whose two kings you are in dread will be deserted. *(Isaiah 7:13-16)*.

Given the context and the timeframe given by Isaiah, most scholars assume—when we read the text at the first level—that the prophet is speaking about Hezekiah. Traditionally, the time for a child to know the difference between right and wrong—the "evil and the good"—is about the age of twelve. So the prophet is telling Ahaz that within twelve years the two nations he is concerned about will no longer even exist but that a new power—Assyria—would rise up to be an even greater threat. But in that time God would anoint a new leader from within the house of Ahaz who would have a different name or reputation than Ahaz. Whereas Ahaz refused to trust God, this new leader would do and be something that Ahaz had failed to do and to be.

He would be Immanuel. He would be a reminder to all the people that God is with us.

King Ahaz lacked the faith to trust God and instead placed his trust in armies and alliances. He calculated the odds and, when push came to shove, he did what he thought was necessary to preserve the nation and save his own position. In the end, however, he lost them both.

Isaiah 36 and 37 tell the story of Hezekiah. In the fourteenth year of his reign, King Sennacherib, the new king of Assyria, came to collect on the debts of Ahaz and threatened to bring his army up against Jerusalem. He sent his messenger to the gates of Jerusalem to threaten the people: "Do not let Hezekiah mislead you by saying, The LORD will save us. Has any of the gods of the nations saved their land out of the hand of the king of Assyria?" (36:18). Chapter 36 of Isaiah contains some of the best trash talk in the Bible.

Hezekiah and Jerusalem were in almost an identical situation to the one that his father, Ahaz, had faced. If the calculations that kept Ahaz from trusting the Lord where overwhelming, the odds that now faced Hezekiah were insurmountable. No nation had been able to stand against Assyria. Judah would be no exception.

But just like his father, Ahaz, Hezekiah received a word from the prophet. Isaiah proclaimed to the shaking and terrified king,

> Thus says the LORD: Do not be afraid because of the words that you have heard, with which the servants of the king of Assyria have reviled me. I myself will put a spirit in him, so that he shall hear a rumor, and return to his own land; I will cause him to fall by the sword in his own land *(Isaiah 37:6-7).*

Ahaz and Hezekiah: similar threat, same message—trust in the Lord—but a different response. Ahaz calculated the threat and then failed to trust in the Lord. Hezekiah in Isaiah 37 took the letter full of Assyrian threats directly to the Temple and spread the letter before the Lord. Laying himself on the ground, he prayed to Yahweh

O LORD of hosts, God of Israel, who are enthroned above the cherubim, you are God, you alone, of all the kingdoms of the earth; you have made heaven and earth. Incline your ear, O LORD and hear; open your eyes O LORD, and see; hear all the words of Sennacherib, which he has sent to mock the living God. Truly, O LORD, the kings of Assyria have laid waste all the nations and their lands, and have hurled their gods into the fire, though they were no gods, but the work of human hands—wood and stone—and so they were destroyed. So now, O LORD our God, save us from his hand, so that all the kingdoms of the earth may know that you alone are the LORD *(Isaiah 37:16-20).*

As he lay before the Lord and leapt in faith and trust in God's deliverance, Hezekiah became what Isaiah expected he would become. He became a reminder to all the people that God is with us. What the people of Judah needed in both the time of Ahaz and Hezekiah was not just a leader who could analyze and calculate the threats that they faced. What they needed was a leader who could help them trust in the Lord and be reminded that God was with them. Ahaz trusted his calculations and ended up making the list of bad kings. Hezekiah laid his calculations before the Lord, trusted in his promises, and became the Immanuel king.

But there is most significantly a second level at which we must read the prophetic expectations. Rightly, Matthew picks up Isaiah's hopes for God's ultimate leader and uses the prophetic words in Isaiah 7 as the ground from which he draws his inspired expectation that "The virgin shall conceive and bear a son, and they shall name him Emmanuel" (Matthew 1:23). Jesus in His life, death, and resurrection is the ultimate fulfillment of God's expectations and the forever reminder that God is with us.

I don't believe, however, that Jesus was without a calculating nature. For me, one of the most significant moments for Jesus in His ministry was in the Garden of Gethsemane as He prayed for strength from the Father. Forgive my imagination, but it helps me to picture Jesus kneeling against a rock with a yellow legal pad with a line drawn down the middle. On one side He has written, "The will of the Father." On the other side He has written, "Compromise and make an alliance with the Pharisees and the principalities and powers." On each side Jesus has done the calculations and realizes that the side of the line oriented toward the Father's will is rapidly leading to rejection, betrayal, and crucifixion. The math simply doesn't work. The options are to let the cup of suffering pass from Him or walk forward, trusting that the one who called Him could raise Him from the dead.

We worship Jesus as Christ and as the fulfillment of all of Israel and Judah's messianic hopes because He was obedient to the will of the Father and in trust He gave himself up to death, believing in the life-giving purposes and power of the Father. So on many, many levels the cross serves as the eternal reminder to humankind that God is with us.

The expectations of the prophets, however, should still be read at a third level. Certainly Christ is the ultimate fulfillment of Isaiah's prophetic hopes. But I am convinced that the words still serve as the holy expectations for the kind of leader God still needs for His people today. He needs women and men who, as Hezekiah and Jesus did, lean hard in trust on Him.

I believe God likes calculators. I believe He is okay with my nature to analyze and assess the risks in nearly every decision. But what He needs from His calculating disciples is the willingness—when He has truly called us—to set aside our calculations and lay ourselves before Him in trust.

We enter the cycle of victorious living by committing our way to the Lord. But we move along in His life of shalom by learning to lean hard in trust upon Him. I am still learning the life of trust. But I believe with all that I am that what the Church needs today is disciples who live in such a way that they remind the people of God of something we too often forget: *God is with us.*

> **I am sure you realize it is possible anywhere along life's journey for fret to set in. Satan will not cease his efforts to get us out of orbit. He usually attacks the mind and seeks to insert insidious little doubts that, if allowed to, will easily start us toward fret. God's call for us not to fret is not only a requirement for entering the cycle but also a requirement for remaining in it. The opportunity to fret will always present itself; but as trust becomes more and more our way of life, we become less aware of the assaults on our faith.** —*Earl Lee*

CHAPTER DISCUSSION QUESTIONS

Chapter 3: Trust: Leapers and Calculators

1. Would you describe yourself as more of a leaper or a calculator? Explain.

_____

_____

_____

_____

2. At what points in your own life do you find it most difficult to trust in the Lord's presence and provision?

_____

_____

_____

_____

3. What is the relationship between trusting in the Lord and responsibly planning for the future?

_____

_____

_____

_____

4. Reflect and write about a season or time in your life (perhaps a time of great trials) when God has reminded you of his faithfulness and presence in your life. If you feel it is appropriate, share your experience with the group.

_____

_____

_____

_____

four

DELIGHT
SNOW CONES FOR EVERYONE

**I believe here is where we have a deep
problem in our cycle. Too often we forget
to rejoice in the Lord. It is a matter of remembering to say, "Thank You." It means
we revere the Giver more than His gift.
... When we delight in the Lord we will lift
up our eyes with deliberate intent; it is a
matter of the will, not the emotions. But
it often refreshingly affects the emotions.**
                                        —Earl Lee

I learned to play baseball in elementary school when my
father was pastoring in Phoenix. Because of the heat, there
were always concession stands next to the Little League
fields with plenty of liquids on hand. At that time the tradi-
tion was that at the end of the game the winning team was
given tickets to be used at the concession stand to receive a
free snow cone as a reward for having played so well. The
members of the losing team were left to go ask their parents for money after the game if they were to share in the

snow cone festivities. It was a long time ago, but I must not have been on many winning teams, because I remember having to ask for snow cone money with great frequency.

We moved away, but during my early high school years we came back to visit friends who had been part of the church and lived in our same area of Phoenix. They had a son who was younger than I who happened to have a Little League game while we were there. On the way to watch his game he informed us all that the league had come up with a new snow cone policy that year. Over the years the parents had come to realize that giving free snow cones to the winning team may have been sending the wrong message to the players, so they decided to give snow cones to both the winners and the losers.

I remember that the game did not go well for my young friend's team. I believe that he struck out every time he was up to bat. But I noticed that even after striking out, he skipped back to the bench. While he was playing defense in the infield, there were several times when the ball went under his glove or between his legs. But he kept smiling and encouraging the other players. Their team lost the game badly, so at the end of the game I went to him in hopes of giving him a pep talk and some encouragement. I had barely started my "Life Saver" speech when he looked up and said, "Don't worry about it, Scott. Both teams get snow cones now!"

I realized that with the change in the concession policy his whole outlook on baseball had changed. When he struck out it did not matter—he was still getting a snow cone. When he made an error in the field, there was nothing to worry about—the frozen treats had already been determined.

Life is certainly more serious now than snow cones for both teams, but I think back often on the deep sense of rejoicing with which he played that game, knowing that the reward at the end would be his, regardless of how he played.

It is my hope that you will not over-read this simple story. I'm fairly certain that God has not predetermined our human end. I do think how we play the game of life matters both today and into eternity. We enter the cycle of victorious living by committing our way to the Lord and trusting in Him. But once we learn to trust in God's sovereign ability to work all things together—even the most difficult and challenging of life's circumstances—for good when we look to Him and are called according to His purpose (Romans 8:28), then we can learn the third step in the cycle: to rejoice or delight in Him. "Take delight in the LORD, and he will give you the desires of your heart" (Psalm 37:4).

In the previous chapter we looked at the lives of Kings Ahaz and Hezekiah as we read about them in Isaiah 1 through 39. I would like to return to Isaiah again, but this time let's reflect on the last section of the great prophetic book: chapters 56—66.

Most Old Testament scholars argue that Isaiah is given to us in three sections. Chapters 1 through 39 address Judah in the time before exile into Babylon (during the reigns of Ahaz and Hezekiah). Chapters 40 through 55 are addressed to the people during exile when the message they need is one of comfort (see Isaiah 40:1) and hope (see Isaiah 40:27-31) as they await God's redemption.

But the last section, chapters 56-66, is addressed to Judah after Cyrus the Persian has released them from their Babylonian captivity. When they get home to Jerusalem, they discover that there isn't much left. In fact, all that remains is rubble. Not one stone in the walls that formed the city was left on top of another. The people were faced with the seemingly insurmountable task of starting over with no wealth or power to draw upon for strength and resource.

We are told about the Judeans' work of rebuilding in books like Ezra, Haggai, and Zechariah. Reconstruction of the city began around 520 B.C. and lasted for at least four years or more. Like the prophet Jonah, God had heard their cries from the belly of Sheol. But also like Jonah, they felt a little as though they had been upchucked back into life. They expected God's powerful redemption. What they got instead was homelessness amidst a pile of rubble.

Yet into their pain and disappointment, the Spirit of God once again inspired the prophet to speak. In Isaiah 61 the people receive this powerful message from the Lord: "The spirit of the Lord GOD is upon me, because the LORD has anointed me; he has sent me to bring good news to the oppressed, to bind up the broken-hearted, to proclaim liberty to the captives, and release to the prisoners; to proclaim the year of the LORD's favour" (Isaiah 61:1-2).

In the Old Testament we find many important economic codes that shaped the day-to-day life of Israel. Three very important laws that the people followed with great regularity were the laws of tithing, gleaning, and Sabbath. Each week and month the people brought ten percent of what they raised and produced to the storehouses so that the priests and the poor would receive what they needed. The gleaning law said that a good Hebrew could not harvest to the very edge of one's field but instead left the outer row and the wide corners unharvested so that the alien and sojourner passing through the land could receive what they needed from the outer edges of one's life. The Sabbath laws made one day a week and one year out of seven holy. This time was set apart for rest and for sharing with God and with one another. These laws were intended to help God's people be a generous people, a hospitable people, and a people who made celebration with one's community—and not work—the end or fullest purpose of life.

Yet even though the people followed these three laws faithfully, there was a fourth economic code connected to the other three that the people did not obey. Leviticus 25 lays out the laws regarding the Year of Jubilee. After the people have celebrated a complete cycle of Sabbatical years—seven sets of seven years; the following year, the fiftieth year, is to be set aside as a year of the Lord's favor. In the Year of Jubilee all the slaves or prisoners (primarily in that state because of debt) are to be released, all the debts are to be cancelled, and all the people who for one reason or another had lost their ancestral land were to receive that land back. The Year of Jubilee was like a giant social and economic "do-over."

Do you remember when you were a child and played with an Etch-a-Sketch? After making a mess on the screen, you could just shake the whole contraption, and all the writing disappeared and you could start all over again. This is the purpose of the Jubilee. Even the most just society needs a do-over from time to time.

Unfortunately, as far as we know, the people of God never obeyed the laws of Jubilee. The prisoners were never released, the debts were never cancelled, and the dispossessed never got their land back. It's not hard to figure out why the people ignored this law. The rich and powerful, in all of their various forms—then and now—have a very difficult time giving their wealth and power back. The philosophy was that if the system has been working, there is no reason to break it.

But when the people went into exile in Babylon, several of the prophets interpreted their exile as God's punishment upon the people for their hard-heartedness and their disobedience to God's purposes, including their unwillingness to enact the Jubilee year of God's favor.

With that background in mind, it brings to light the profound proclamation of the prophet in Isaiah 61. The Spirit of the Lord is upon the prophet to proclaim the good news of Jubilee. This good news means that the prisoners are released, the debt of rebellion is cancelled, and the people get to go home. What the people see as rubble the prophet sees as God giving the people a do-over. It may mean a lot of work, but in a sense the prophet believes that God has shaken the Etch-a-Sketch for Judah and given them the opportunity to start all over again. The rebuilding project of Jerusalem is not a time for despair but a time to rejoice in the Lord and the new thing He is doing in His people.

As the prophet continues his oracle of joy, he proclaims that Judah will no longer be the lesser child among the nations but that they will inherit the double portion of the inheritance that was regularly given to the firstborn child in a family. In verses 3-4 he pronounces three important "insteads" over them:

The Lord will give his people—

- A garland *instead of* ashes,
- The oil of gladness *instead of* mourning,
- The mantle of praise *instead of* a faint spirit (emphasis added).

He also proclaims three "theys" upon them:

- *They* will be called oaks of righteousness, the planting of the Lord, to display his glory.
- *They* shall build up the ancient ruins, they shall raise up the former devastations;
- *They* shall repair the ruined cities, the devastation of many generations.

Can you see it now? Through the prophet's Spirit-empowered eyes the ruins are not a reason for despair but a reason to rejoice. God is doing something entirely new with His people. They can rejoice because He is turning the sorrow they experienced in Babylon, when they believed they had no future, into the joyful celebration of the now-open future they have been given by God's grace. They can rejoice, because when God is done with them they will be solid as oak trees, completely rebuilt in newness, and their previous devastations will be only a memory. This isn't just good news. This is *great* news!

So how should the people respond to the prophet's insight? They should rejoice. Isaiah 61:10 tells the story: "I will greatly rejoice in the LORD, my whole being shall exult in my God; for he has clothed me with the garments of salvation, he has covered me with the robe of righteousness, as a bridegroom decks himself with a garland, and as a bride adorns herself with her jewels."

The theme of God's redemption of Judah continues into the next chapter of the prophet's proclamation. Isaiah 62:4 states that the nation will get a whole new identity. They will no longer be called Azubah (meaning *Forsaken*) and their land will no longer be referred to as Shemamah (meaning *Desolate*), but they will now be called Hephzibah (meaning *My Delight Is in Her*), and their land will be called Beulah (meaning *Married*). The celebration that should take place is like the party that goes on at a wedding. The lonely woman who thought no one would ever love her and care for her has been wooed and is now marrying the most powerful ruler in the land. Rejoice! Redemption is underway. The prophet wants the people to get ready for the party to end all parties. Free snow cones for everybody!

We find the way of God's shalom through commitment and trust, but we stay in the way by learning to delight and rejoice in what He has done, what He is doing, and what He is going to do. Fret is the exit ramp out of the victorious life. Learning to delight in the Lord is the glue that keeps us tied close to His heart.

Delighting in the Lord is not a naïve ideal that allows us to conclude that we will always feel happy or that we will never face suffering or sadness. Part of our calling as disciples is to weep with one another. To delight in the Lord is to have that deep-rooted sense in the core of our being that we are God's children and that His sovereign love has the last word, even in the face of death. Like the feelings of love that are renewed out of the commitment of married partners to love each other for better or for worse, for richer or for poorer, in sickness and in health, so, too, the feelings associated with delight return to us out of the deep-rooted quality of joy in knowing that in all things God is at work.

So rejoice. Delight in the Lord. Play the game of life with passion and joy. Play as though the game depends upon you, while knowing that it ultimately depends upon He who is at work in you.

John Philip Sousa, known as "the march king," was surprised one day to hear floating up into his hotel room the strains of his

favorite march, "The Stars and Stripes Forever." It was being played in a slow, lazy, dragging manner by an organ grinder in the street below.

He dashed down into the street. "Here, here!" he called to the sleepy organ grinder. "That is no way to play my march!"

He seized the handle and turned it vigorously. The music came out spirited and happy, and the little organ grinder smiled and bowed low to Mr. Sousa.

The next night Mr. Sousa heard his song again, and this time the tempo was right. He looked out his window and noticed a large sign over the organ with the grinder's name on it and underneath the words "Pupil of John Philip Sousa."

If we ever learn to delight in the Lord—and we must—we will write under the joys of our lives, "Pupil of Jesus Christ."

—Earl Lee

CHAPTER DISCUSSION QUESTIONS

Chapter 4: Delight: Snow Cones for Everyone

1. How do you understand the author's story about "snow cones for everyone" in regard to delighting in the Lord?

2. Do you believe it is possible to delight in the Lord in the midst of tragedy, suffering, and loss? Explain.

3. What do you believe to be the most common barriers that keep people from delighting in the Lord?

4. Who is a brother or sister in Christ (living or deceased) who has demonstrated to you what it looks like to genuinely delight in the Lord throughout his or her life?

five

REST
BEARING THE YOKE OF CHRIST

> The rest I speak about is an active rest.
> He speaks; I listen and obey. And with each
> new situation I find my way through the
> cycle to inner rest. It is a rest from friction,
> not a rest from action. . . . There is a rest in
> doing when it is in the Lord. We should be
> sure to differentiate between ease and rest.
> —*Earl Lee*

My two favorite Hebrew words occur in the opening chapter of the Bible. They are the almost twin words *tohu* and *bohu*. In most translations of Genesis they are interpreted as "formless" and "void." The creation hymn that opens the Scripture begins this way: "In the beginning when God created the heavens and the earth, the earth was *tohu* and *bohu*. . . . "

These two words are always connected, and they are more than just descriptions of the nothingness—the *ex nihilo*—prior to God's creative activity. They are words that epitomize for the Hebrew people the forces in the world that try to undo the order that God desires. They are the enemies of order. *Tohu* and *bohu* could easily be translated as "chaos," and they are usually associated with water. Water is certainly a necessity for life, and there are many good forms of water in the Bible. But large bodies of water are frequently sources of threat and destruction for ancient people. Think about the pictures of devastation as the tsunami waves rushed across the landscape of Japan in March 2011, and you will start to understand how the ancient Hebrews thought about *tohu* and *bohu*. These ugly forces are the names God's people give to the chaos that undoes the goodness in life.

You will have to forgive my imagination again, but when I read Genesis 1 I often picture a seven-round World Wrestling Federation match. Picture, if you will, the microphone dropping down from the ceiling and the black-tied announcer stepping to the middle of the cosmic fight ring. "Ladies and gentlemen!" he shouts. "It is the beginning! So let's get ready to rumble!"

In one corner the announcer directs the audience's attention to a massive, ugly, mask-wearing wrestler, complete with cape and tights. When he introduces the reigning champion—Tohu Bohu—the crowd boos, hisses, and throws popcorn at the dreaded enemy. The champion snarls and spits and makes ugly gestures back to the cosmic spectators.

But then the unseen opponent of the prince of chaos is introduced. The crowd grows silent as the announcer proclaims, "In every other corner, we have our challenger. He's omnipotent. He's omniscient. He's omnipresent. He's God Almighty. He's Yahweh!" The crowd erupts into cheers as they await the ultimate battle between the loving, compassionate Creator and the dark, ugly forces of un-creation.

My WWF imagery may sound a bit farfetched, but notice how the presence of God is introduced in the text. "The earth was formless and void [*tohu* and *bohu*] and darkness covered the face of the deep, while a wind from God swept over the face of the waters" (Genesis 1:2). The Hebrew word for wind is the word *ruach* (you have to say it from the back of the throat—Ru-ACH). This fascinating word is the same word used for God's Spirit. It is very important that "wind" and "Spirit" come from the same word. It helps us make sense of the sound of a mighty wind that filled the disciples' upper room on the day of Pentecost. But notice in this second verse in Genesis that it is God's Spirit hovering over the waters—ready to take on the chaos.

The first three rounds—or three days—of the creation battle all center on the same basic word: "separation." On each of the first three days, as God speaks the creation into existence, the end result is the same: something gets separated from something else. On day one God speaks light into existence, and then He *separates* the light from the dark. The light is called "day," and the darkness is called "night." The second day, God places a dome in the midst of the waters of chaos and *separates* the water above the dome from the water that is below the dome. The water above the dome is called "sky," and eventually the water below the dome is called "seas." Day three, dry land appears. In gathering together the various bodies of water, God *separates* the dry land from the oceans.

The cosmic WWF match is almost half completed. The battle has been waged for three rounds, and the *tohu bohu* is not doing very well. In fact, it might be correct to say that the *tohu* has been defeated. Because the first three days are spent forming all things, the word *tohu* is frequently translated as "formless." But after only three days of creation, formlessness is no longer a problem. All things have been formed through God's gracious acts of separation.

Now it's time for Yahweh to waylay the *bohu.* The bell rings for round four and God gets going by creating the sun, the moon, and the stars and *filling* the dome of the sky with all of these amazing lights. On day five God pounds the *bohu* by *filling* the sky with birds and *filling* the seas with swarms of water creatures. And to finish off His utter defeat of the *bohu,* He spends day six *filling* the land with living creatures of every kind and most significantly creating humankind in His image.

As you read Genesis 1, I hope you will notice the way the days fit together. Days one through three all have to do with forming the formless (the *tohu*). And days four through six have to do with filling the emptiness or void (the *bohu*). I also think it is beautiful that what God separates on day one (the light and dark), He fills on day four (with the sun, moon, and stars). What He separates on day two (sea and sky), He fills on day five (with birds and fish). And what He separates on day three (dry land), He fills on day six (with animals and humans).

When the bell rings for the seventh and final round, the *tohu bohu* does not answer. The final day of God's creative act is the day of rest, the day of shalom, the day of blessing. For the Hebrew people, the pinnacle of creation is the Sabbath. God's intentions for humankind are most fully revealed in the Sabbath rest. It is God's purpose for all of creation to live at peace with Him and at peace with one another. God's desire for the creation is for it to be free from *tohu bohu* so that it can be a place of His shalom.

Of course, in the Genesis narratives chapter one is not the end of the story for the forces of chaos. Essentially, through sin and violence, humankind reawakens the powers of destruction. Think, for example, how significant the story of Noah is in the light of how *tohu bohu* and the waters of chaos are connected. In the account of Noah, God again has to use His *ruach* to blow the waters back to where they belong and continue His work of creating shalom for His people.

But returning to Genesis 1, I think the three words that embody God's creation process are extremely significant: "separation," "filling," and "rest" or "blessing." These words seem to frequently accompany God's purposes for His people in the Scriptures.

For example, God calls Abraham to *separate* himself from his original places of security and provision and be blessed or *filled* by God's presence so that he and his descendants could be a blessing of shalom and *rest* to all the nations of the world.

In the New Testament the Greek word for Church— *Ecclesia*—literally means "called-out ones." Disciples of Jesus inevitably are called out of the world. We are called to be *separate* from the principalities and powers present in the world. The purpose of being called out is to be *filled* in unique ways by God's presence or Spirit. But separation and filling are not for their own sake. God's people are separated and filled in order to be—as is the Sabbath day itself—a blessing of peace and *rest* to the entire creation.

King David rightly points us to God's final purposes by urging us to "Be still before the LORD, and wait patiently for him" (Psalm 37:7).

The great invitation that Jesus gives His disciples is "Come to me, all you that are weary and are carrying heavy burdens, and I will give you rest. Take my yoke upon you, and learn form me; for I am gentle and humble in heart, and you will find rest for your souls. For my yoke is easy, and my burden is light" (Matthew 11:28-30).

Jesus invites people into God's Sabbath rest through himself. He is the way of rest and peace. It is not the strong that Christ invites to himself. It is the weak. The invitation for rest is to those who are finally worn out from running in the way of the Gentiles, in the way of destruction.

It should not surprise us, given that the first three words that embody the cycle of victorious living are action words—commit, trust, and rejoice—that Jesus offers His disciples rest by offering to His followers a yoke. Offering a yoke to the weary seems more than a little out of place. A yoke is an instrument of work. Jesus seems to be offering to those worn out from striving in their own strength more work to do. That's certainly not the case.

When Jesus offers us rest, He is not offering us a vacation, although we may need one from time to time. He is not offering us a withdrawal from life but a whole new way of living. In the first century when a Jewish student left home and followed a rabbi or teacher, it was often referred to as "taking the yoke" of that particular rabbi. The students willfully tied their lives to their teachers and learned a new way of living by connecting themselves—like two oxen yoked together—to their master.

This is likely why Jesus invites His disciples to take on His yoke and learn from Him. Notice Jesus does not invite His followers to learn *about* Him but to learn *from* Him. This invitation is a call to relationship with Christ. Living in the victorious way of Jesus is not just learning rules—or even memorizing four key words—it is finally about being connected to the Lord of life.

A yoke of rest and peace is not a sitting instrument. It is a walking instrument. As we walk through the ups and downs of life with Jesus, we learn His gentle ways, and we are renewed in the deepest aspects of who we are. In Him we find the rest our souls crave.

I think it could be argued that of all the Old Testament laws—with the exception of love for God and love for neighbor—the Sabbath laws were most important to Israel. The keeping of the Sabbath was the way they marked their lives as unique from all the other nations around them.

There is an outdoor shopping area in Beverly Hills, California, where my wife and I like to go and people watch; we can't afford to buy anything there. When we go it is usually Friday evening or Saturday morning. There are several synagogues and a number of Orthodox Jewish neighborhoods close to the area where we hang out. The faithful in those neighborhoods will not drive their cars on the Sabbath, so from sundown on Friday through sundown on Saturday they can be seen in their hats, yarmulkes, and prayer shawls walking back and forth to synagogue services. It is fascinating to see a distinct people, living in the midst of the opulence and over-the-top conspicuous consumption of Beverly Hills, keeping their unique way of life alive by resting on the Sabbath.

A few years ago when Al Gore and Jewish Congressman Joe Lieberman were the Democratic candidates for president and vice-president, I saw my favorite political bumper sticker of all time. It read, "Gore and Lieberman in 2000: We'll Work for You 24/6." I hope you get the Sabbath joke.

As much as I deeply admire the commitment to Sabbath-keeping that marks the lives of some of my Jewish neighbors in Los Angeles as unique to the world, I am not convinced that a legalistic ceasing from working or driving for a twenty-four-hour period of time is what God fully intended to be the uniqueness of His people. We Protestant Christians may need to take more seriously the practices that go into being a people of rest, but I think it is the *quality* of shalom—the state of rest in our souls with God and others—that significantly marks our uniqueness as God's people in the world.

Again, to rest in God is not to be free from stress. But it does mean that our lives are rooted in the love of God in ways that give us stability in the midst of the storms of life.

Rest in God is the stability of life that the prophet Jeremiah is referring to when he speaks of how blessed are those who trust in the Lord:

They shall be like a tree planted by water sending out its roots by the stream. It shall not fear when heat comes, and its leaves shall stay green; in the year of drought it is not anxious, and it does not cease to bear fruit (Jeremiah 17:8).

Rest in God is the stability Jesus refers to in the Sermon on the Mount when He speaks about the wise man who builds his house on the rock of obedience to His words:

The rain fell, the floods came, and the winds blew and beat on that house, but it did not fall, because it had been founded on rock *(Matthew 7:25)*.

Rest in God is the quality of life that great hymn writer Horatio Spafford was referring to when out of his own pain of loss he wrote the great words

When peace like a river attendeth my way,
When sorrows like sea billows roll.
Whatever my lot, Thou hast taught me to say,
"It is well, it is well with my soul."

Fret and worry mark the lives of those caught in the cycle of brokenness that defines so much of the world today. But God's way for His people—His cycle of victorious living—begins in commitment, continues in trust, finds life in rejoicing, and gives to His disciples the benefit of His rest. It is well with our souls.

> **Rest not only means readiness and expectation but also implies a steady satisfaction. The work of God's grace in sanctifying the believer has long been described as the establishing grace whereby one is established in God's rest and is satisfied for life to be this way. Paul was nearing the end of his earthly life and expressed his satisfaction with these words: "But none of these things move me, neither count I my life dear unto myself, so that I might finish my course with joy, and the ministry, which I have received of the Lord Jesus, to testify the gospel of the grace of God" (Acts 20:24, KJV). God's rest brings great inner peace.**
> **—*Earl Lee***

CHAPTER DISCUSSION QUESTIONS

Chapter 5: Rest: Snow Bearing the Yoke of Christ

1. What does the author mean by an "active rest?"

_____

_____

2. How is "shalom" the pinnacle of God's creation?

_____

_____

3. How is sin and violence the antithesis of God's created order?

_____

_____

4. The author mentions the reoccurring themes of separation, filling, rest, and blessing. Where do you see these themes in scripture and in the Christian life?

_____

_____

5. How would you describe the distinction between learning about Jesus and learning from Jesus?

_____

_____

6. How can we as God's children experience shalom in a world full of demanding schedules, smart phones, noise, and so on?

_____

_____

six

A TALE
OF TWO PRINCESSES

"Jesus is Lord" is the great center of the
cycle of victorious living. The key phrase
from each of these four verses in Psalm 37
is "in the Lord," "Commit thy way unto the
Lord"; "Trust in the Lord"; "Delight . . . in
the Lord"; "Rest in the Lord." This kind of
living demands a sacramental view of life
where everything is done unto the Lord.
—*Earl Lee*

God has a way of life He wants His people to find. It is the
way of His shalom. It is the way of the righteous. It is the
cycle of His victorious living. Fret is one of the major exit
ramps out of the victorious life. Commitment to the Lord-
ship of Christ is always the road back into the life God has
for you. Staying in the right life requires that the disciple of
Jesus lean hard in trust upon His loving and gracious character and nature. Realizing what Christ is doing in and
through us as we walk with Him gives us reason to rejoice
and delight in Him. And as we walk in the way, our lives

are marked by the quiet strength and stability that comes with the ability to rest in His sovereign goodness and love.

That sounds easy doesn't it? Well, it is and it isn't. For some reason—I'm guessing it's our sin—we have a hard time finding and staying squarely within the cycle of God's purpose and peace.

In the Old Testament the hardheartedness of God's people kept leading them astray. Even though there was no eternal quality of life in idols made by hands, the people kept finding themselves being lured away into the worship of idols. Idolatry is always about making a god in our own image. The gods of the Old Testament are almost always associated with fertility and abundance. We keep running after gods who will make life about *us* and will keep our storehouses full. But that life always leads to slavery. It always leads to violence. It always leads to fret, because we realize that we are solely responsible for making our lives count. It always leads to oppression of others and ultimately loss of everything.

In the New Testament Jesus tells us that the road to life is narrow and few find it, while the road to destruction is broad and many choose it for themselves (Matthew 7:13-14). It is so hard for disciples to embrace the irony that when we try to find life in ourselves, we end up losing life; but when we lose our lives for the sake of Christ and His kingdom, we find ourselves.

In the summer of 1997 the world stopped to pay attention as two of the most widely known and deeply beloved women in the world died just a week apart. Princess Diana, loved around the world because of her style, her rags-to-riches story, and her great charitable work, was tragically killed in a car accident while being chased by paparazzi.

Just a few days later, and far less dramatically, Mother Teresa of Calcutta died of natural causes after decades of work among the poorest of the poor in India.

The world rightly stopped to eulogize them both. Because of the proximity of their deaths, commentators couldn't help but compare their lives.

Diana lived the latter half of her life literally as royalty among royalty. Through her marriage to Prince Charles of England she had received worldwide fame and the financial means to do whatever she wanted for the rest of her life. But despite seemingly having it all, the frequent refrain after her death was that despite her wealth and notoriety, happiness eluded her.

Mother Teresa, on the other hand, died with very little in terms of material wealth. In her convent cell she left two worn saris or habits and an old pair of sandals. And yet what the world could not understand is how she lived the life she had committed to with such contentment and joy. Frequently over the years I have watched interviews with Mother Teresa. At some point in the conversation the newscasters would inevitably ask her for her life secret. They would ask questions such as *How do you care for the poor every day? How did you, a nun from one of the poorest corners of the planet, win the Nobel Peace Prize and make such a big difference in the world? How did you find such contentment and peace?*

Her answer was almost always the same. She would smile and say, "I've tried my best never to say no to Jesus."

Princess Diana had nearly everything but rarely found happiness. Mother Teresa had almost nothing and found the secret to contentment.

Princess Diana had a life that almost no one can have but to which nearly everyone aspires.

Mother Teresa had a life that everyone could have but to which very few aspire.

Even though it has yet to lead to abundant life, the world keeps running after the way of the empire, the way of the wicked, the way of the Gentiles, the way of the self. The Lord is inviting us to the way of shalom, the way of the Kingdom, the way of Christ.

The victorious way of life is entered through *commitment* to the Lord.

It is maintained through *trust* in the Lord.

It is sustained by *delighting* in the Lord.

And it is fulfilled in *resting* in the Lord.

My prayer is that with the psalmist you will find the victorious way of life that God has for all of His people.

> **So now we move on, and the adventure of life in the cycle never ends. There will be new insights, new joys, new discoveries; for really, this total concept is only my way of describing our walk with Jesus Christ. It is life on tip-toes of excitement in the Spirit. ... Jesus is Lord!** —*Earl Lee*

CHAPTER DISCUSSION QUESTIONS

Chapter 6: A Tale of Two Princesses

1. How does a life marked by selfish gain inevitably lead to slavery?

_____

_____

_____

_____

2. Who are some other people who have exemplified the victorious way of life that you have known or heard of? What did they do?

_____

_____

_____

_____

3. What are some ways you have been challenged in the previous five weeks of this study?

_____

_____

_____

_____

4. What are some changes you have made or need to make in order to embody the victorious way of living?

_____

_____

_____

_____

1971 Original Text of
The Cycle of Victorious Living

by Earl G. Lee

To those who have meant the most to me
in my walk with Christ and its development:

My wife, Hazel

My children, Gary, Gayle, and Grant

Contents

Preface

While on deputation work after my second term as a missionary in India I entered into a new level of life in the Spirit. Due to the nudging of the Spirit, I knew before I left India that I would not be returning for a third term. This revelation was extremely jolting for two reasons: I loved India and she had become a satisfying way of life for me; also, facing a new direction in my middle years was not easy. As our ship drew away from India's shores I can still see a fellow missionary making the sign of the cross with her hands. Little did she know how appropriate was her farewell.

"What are your plans for the future?" was the question I faced repeatedly during those deputation days. I tried to explain the unusual direction of the Spirit's guidance in my life, but people's baffled looks added to my increasing frustration. It did not make sense—and I became a bit desperate in my spirit.

During the month of October 1960, while on a missionary tour in Oklahoma, I told the Lord I needed a settled spirit, a sure promise. The answer I received was so quietly simple I hardly knew God had spoken. His word to me was "You *have* My will for today; I will take care of tomorrow."

I felt great inner relaxation as God brought my living to its least common denominator. His will for the day! That was all that was necessary. Although it would be over nine months before I was to have any idea what the future held for me and my family, I had entered into a new level of living much like ships go from one lock to another in a canal. It was a move upward in my spirit, and the truths that came to me through this experience I have called *the cycle of victorious living.*

Although this fresh insight could have come to me through the writings of Paul or the teachings of Christ, it opened up to me through the thirty-seventh psalm.

In order to clarify the truth, I have devised the diagram below. A glance at it shows the smooth sequence of living in a spiritual orbit. *Fret* is always the way out of orbit. With a bit of change of scriptural sequence we stay in the cycle by *committing, trusting, delighting,* and finally *resting.* Jesus Christ is the great Center of victorious living. The phrase "in the Lord" is the key thought. As I try to explain these truths more fully in the following chapters, I trust many will enter into a new level of dynamic, Spirit-filled life in Christ.

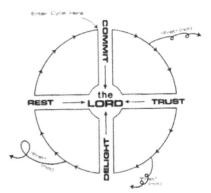

Fret Not

Last year I was asked by a religious organization to speak on the subject of victorious living. Due to a printer's error, the subject was announced as "The Cycle of *Victorian* Living." I was quite amused as I read the card. No, it is not *Victorian* living. It is not a life of continual negatives, prohibitions, inhibitions, and long-faced unimpressiveness. People who live out their lives "in quiet desperation" are a part of the problem of religious life today rather than a part of the solution. They fret. God wants us to be free from continual fretting. We need to unravel some of the tangles in our thinking and realize how completely free God wants us to be. He has made provision for abundant living through the power of the Holy Spirit in the fully yielded heart.

He is not teasing us when He tells us not to fret, but it is quite possible that there is some confusion as to the meaning of the word *fret*. What one may call "fret" others may call "legitimate concern," or the opposite may be true. Yet it is amazing how the Holy Spirit can guide us through a maze of semantics into vital truth. He does not wish our spiritual life to become frayed no matter how we interpret words. *Fret not* is more than a pastoral platitude; it is a divine imperative.

Now David faced a legitimate concern. You would think he had access to one of our daily newspapers as he wrote about the ungodly prospering and evildoers standing in the way of the righteous. His psalms are full of these observations. But his opening admonition in Psalm 37 is *Fret not.*

In writing to the Philippians, Paul said, "Be careful for nothing." Or, as the *Living New Testament* translates it, "Don't worry about anything; instead, pray about everything; tell God your needs and don't forget to thank Him for His answers. If you do this you will experience God's peace, which is far more wonderful than the human mind can understand. His peace will keep your thoughts and your hearts quiet and at rest as you trust in Christ Jesus." Over and over again we are pointed to the great Center, Christ Jesus.

Paul did not write these words from the Huntington-Sheraton Hotel. He was in jail. But the entire letter to the Philippians sounds as if Paul had found his cycle of victorious living while in a dungeon. He uses such phrases as "Be careful for nothing"; "I trust in the Lord"; "I can do all things through Christ"; "Rejoice in the Lord alway"; "The peace of God shall be with you"; "I have all, and abound"; "My God shall supply all your need"; "I have learned, in whatsoever state I am, therewith to be content"; "Now unto God and our Father be glory for ever and ever."

The teachings of Jesus have the same familiar ring: "Seek ye first the kingdom of God"; "Take no thought for the morrow"; "Lay up for yourselves treasures in heaven"; "Consider the lilies of the field"; "Ask, and it shall be given you; seek, and ye shall find; knock, and it shall be opened unto you."

Oswald Chambers says, "All our fret and worry is caused by calculating without God." It destroys victorious living as surely as insects and other pests destroy leaves.

I enjoy caring for my roses, camellias, and azaleas. I had one very anemic camellia bush off in a corner of the flower bed. Weeds had sprung up around it, and although it gave a few weak blooms, I determined to restore its beauty. As I cleaned out the weeds, I discovered the true cause for concern. Embedded in the soil near the roots and on up under the leaves were a number of well-fed snails. I heartily disliked their intrusion and decided then and there they would have to go if I was to have a healthy camellia bush. With the use of specially prepared pellets, they were done away with. The blooms have been rich and colorful ever since.

Fret is the snail under the leaf, and in order to have lives of fragrance and beauty, these snails of fret must go. And God has a specially prepared way for their exit. It is found in the cycle of victorious living!

Tension is normal and natural in life. Without tension we could not exist any more than a violin string can be played without being stretched across the bridge. This creative tension is not the same thing as destructive worry. Worry is like racing an automobile engine while it is in neutral. The gas and noise and smog do not get us anywhere. But legitimate concern (creative tension) is putting the car into low gear on your way to moving ahead. You tell yourself that you are going to use the power God has given you to do something about the situation that could cause you to fret. One really moves into high gear when he affirms, "Now unto him that is able to do exceeding abundantly above all that we ask or think, according to the power that worketh in us, unto him be glory." That scripture goes places, and you go with it. It's a long way from worrying, fretting, and stewing in a state of paralysis. Maybe you are like I am. When I know there is something that needs to be done, or someone I need to see, I am miserable until I take care of the matter. Fret, usually, is not removed by praying but by doing. One has to take the gear shift out of neutral, put it into "low," and get going.

Dr. E. Stanley Jones tells about a bird in India which he calls a champion pessimist. This bird goes around all day crying shrilly, "Pity-to-do-it, pity-to-do-it"; and at night, they say, he sleeps on his back with his long legs in the air to keep the sky from falling!

Too often we excuse ourselves by saying, "Well, I'm just a natural worrywart!" But let me tell you, if you examine the worrywart you will find his malady is malignant. It eats down into the spirit until it destroys life. The only way to handle this critical malignancy is to let the Holy Spirit operate on it—because FRET TAKES US OUT OF ORBIT. It is the cell malfunctioning, refusing to work with the normal, happily functioning body cells. It has become self-centered and its refusal to cooperate can bring death. The symptom must be treated speedily and faced with a ruthless honesty. There can be no amateur approach to this deep need. It takes a specialist to handle a malignancy, and the Holy Spirit is the Great Specialist. But He can operate only on the yielded spirit, and the anesthetic is grace.

Someone has described fret as "spiritual heartburn." Most of us can understand that description. Here is a dictionary definition for fret: "To eat away, to gnaw, to gall, to vex, to worry, to agitate, to wear away." Jesus tells us in Mark 4:19 (Moffat): "But the worries of the world . . . come in to choke the word." I have made my own acrostic definition for the word fret. It is:

*F*ever

*R*esentment

*E*nvy

*T*ension (destructive)

Sometimes Charlie Brown can be quite a theologian. In one cartoon we see Linus dragging his blanket as he observes, "You look kinda' depressed, Charlie Brown." Charlie replies, "I worry about school a lot." Then he adds, "I worry about my worrying so much about school." They sit on a log together, and Charlie makes his final observation: "My anxieties have anxieties!" After I used this illustration about Charlie Brown in one of my Sunday sermons, I received the following letter:

DEAR PASTOR LEE,

I want to say, Praise the Lord, while it is fresh in my heart. I have been troubled by a verse for some time now. *The New English Bible* in Phil. 4:5-6 says, "The Lord is near; have no anxiety, but in everything make your requests known to God in prayer and petition, with thanksgiving." God knows that I have been torn by anxiety over insignificant things. Your quote from Snoopy about worrying about worry seemed to fit me. Your message on *Fret Not* was for me. I placed all my worrying and fretting on the altar and left it there, glory be to God! I now claim the above verse, for I have come to realize that it is the second part, "with thanksgiving" and praise, that makes the first part reality.

In Christ,

Naturally, this letter warmed my heart. It is a deep thrill when the sheep go into greener pastures. How wonderful to realize that "all God's commandments are enablings"! Our Heavenly Father never asks us to do what He does not help us, through His grace, to do. It is a loving, providing Father who says, "Don't fret." He wants us to move up into more abundant living above the smog-filled atmosphere of fret.

I am not proposing an impossible way of life. I am not saying one will never fret. But I do maintain there is a cycle of victorious living, a working in and a working out of 1 Corinthians, chapter 13, whereby life ever has an upbeat. When we realize we are becoming victims of fret, that we are getting out of orbit, we ask forgiveness and get back into the cycle by once more committing our way unto the Lord.

CHAPTER TWO

Commit—Hands Down

David says, "Commit thy way unto the LORD; trust also in him; and he shall bring it to pass." Or as Robert Young translates it, "He worketh." David also adds, "He shall bring forth thy righteousness as the light, and thy judgment as the noonday." It all starts with commitment.

Commitment is something other than a sentimental decision that may change one's life for a few emotion-filled days. It is a valid act of the will changing one's whole way of life. It is one's entrance into the cycle of victorious living.

The true meaning of the word *commit* came to me as I was reading this passage in Marathi, our "stepmother" tongue of India. If I were to make a free translation of the Marathi, it says, "Turn what you are and what you have over to God—palms down!" Suppose I hold a piece of chalk in my hand and ask you to take it. You reach out and take it from my upturned hand. But commitment means that we turn our palms over and completely drop what we hold. Nothing of it sticks to our hands. This process involves an exercise of the will. It reminds me of Oswald Chambers' words "I have nothing to do with what will happen if I obey. I must abandon myself to God's call in unconditional surrender and smilingly wash my hands of the consequences." This prayer goes beyond "You take it" to "I release it." There's quite a difference.

It is the prayer I made that day in Oklahoma when I entered into a new level of Spirit-filled living.

Commitment is both initial and continuous. We enter the cycle by commitment. The need, the problem, the urgent prayer request are all given over to God. But one's mind remains quite active, and here is where Satan comes in to accuse. He has not been called "the accuser of the brethren" for nothing! Whenever the temptation to fret assails us, we must tell our adversary that the bothersome matter is now in God's hands and he is wasting his time in needling us.

Satan is not omniscient; he has to be told that we mean business. "Resist the devil, and he will flee." Send him to your great Advocate, Jesus Christ. Jesus knows the set of your heart, the direction of your will, and He also knows how to protect you and how to help you handle your emotions. The will has often been likened to the rudder of a boat. But have you thought of how much more boat there is than rudder? Our emotions make up most of our conscious being, but as Fenelon says, our will to obey God is where true religion resides.

If I were being troubled by someone who was out to destroy my reputation and I had placed my case in the hands of a competent lawyer, I would not waste time talking to my adversary; I would speedily refer him to my lawyer. When you are tempted to relive all the pre-commitment days, the pain and the struggle, and feel the slight edge of doubt moving in, remember the telephone number of your Advocate and put in your call: "Thank You, Lord . . . I believe!"

I like Osterly's translation of the Hebrew for *commit*. He says, "It takes on the idea of to roll, whirl, turn . . . the wholehearted flinging of one's self upon God, knowing that *His will prevails.*"

I was interested in reading about Dr. J. Edwin Orr's experience in commitment. As he was struggling to be filled with the Spirit, he prayed, "Now, Lord, I will give You my business." Nothing happened. As he was also in the throes of making a decision concerning a life's companion, he added, "Lord, I will give her to You." Still nothing happened. One day, in desperation, he cried, "Lord, I give You my choice of a career." Still nothing happened. Finally he completely let go and prayed, "Lord, I give You myself. I commit to You my will, and You have *me.*" Then the Holy Spirit came in cleansing power.

True commitment means we wash our hands of ourselves and give to Him our all—totally, not on condition. When conditions are attached, our palms are held upward; but deep commitment means *our palms are down.* It is the only way to enter the cycle of victorious living. It demands faith in the character of our God and not in the circumstances we see or understand. Oswald Chambers reminds us that we command what we understand.

But as has been stated, commitment is not only initial; it is continuous. We are human beings, not pieces of crystal. We face new situations constantly, and over and over new problems are fed into the cycle. But the process, once learned, becomes a glorious way of life. New light comes, and specific areas are dealt with. You never "arrive" or cease to learn and apply principles of victory. This is practical, sanctified living.

I came across an illustration of commitment in the newspaper back in 1964. A man by the name of Robert Atwood wrote an article for the *Daily Times* of Anchorage, Alaska, describing the terrible earthquake that occurred on Good Friday of that year. He arrived home from work about 5:30 in the evening and his wife was leaving for the grocery store. He hesitated a moment as he considered going with her but decided to remain home and practice his trumpet, as the house would be empty. (Not a bad idea for people who blow trumpets!) Now, in Mr. Atwood's words:

I began practicing my trumpet when the earthquake started. Minor earthquakes are not uncommon here, but they've always taught me to stop what I'm doing and watch what happens. It was quickly obvious that this was no minor earthquake. The chandelier, made from a ship's wheel, swayed too much. Things were falling that had never fallen before. I headed for the door carrying my trumpet. At the door I saw the wall weaving. On the driveway I turned and watched my house swerve and groan as though in mortal agony. It was as though someone had engaged it in a gigantic taffy pull—stretching it, shrinking and twisting it. I became aware of tall trees falling in our yard, so I moved to a spot that I thought would be safe. As I moved I saw cracks appear in the earth. Pieces of ground in jigsaw shapes moved up and down, tilted at all angles.

As I started to climb the fence to my neighbor's yard, the fence disappeared. Trees were falling in crazy patterns. Deep chasms cushioned the impact. I was on the verge of a quick burial. I could not pull my right arm from the sand. It was buried to the shoulder. Most of the rest of my body was also covered. *I had to let go of my trumpet* and my arm pulled free easily!

That story got to me. Too often our trumpets are the expression of our rights, our egos, our desire for recognition and reward; but when we commit our way, we commit ourselves and thus we learn to live without trumpets. "Take my yoke upon you, and learn of me; for I am meek and lowly in heart: and ye shall find rest into your souls."

It may take an earthquake upheaval to pry us loose from our trumpets but it is the only way that will lead to rest of soul.

A short time ago I was working with a weeping seeker at the altar. After a few moments she confessed that her mother was hindering her in her newly discovered way of life. I had preached recently on the cycle of victorious living and asked her if she had heard the sermon. She answered a faint "Yes."

"Do you believe it?" I asked.

"Yes, Pastor, I do," was her reply.

"Then, Betty, I believe what you have to do is to commit your mother, as she is now, to the Lord. Place her in His hands without any condition. Then leave her there. Will you do this?"

I saw a light break over her drawn face as she answered, "I will do just that—now!"

After her prayer I reminded her that the Lord was in charge of her mother and she herself should begin to delight in the Lord and rest.

She began to thank the Lord right there and left the altar having stepped into the cycle.

I met her a week later, and she said to me, "Believe me, delighting in the Lord was the way for me and my sister to live with my mother!" It works! And it begins with commitment. The call to commitment is not from any man. It is God's call to us. His call is always total.

He does not deal in partial victories nor will He be able to do much with halfhearted surrenders. Trumpets have to go. Palms have to be turned down and fully opened.

Elizabeth Burns (nee Gert Behanna), in the story of her life, *The Late Liz,* writes about her son Allen, who rejected her long before she became a Christian and who refused all of her overtures after her conversion. He had caused her much heartache. She had wept over him far into the night and wondered if God could ever bring all the pieces together. She writes,

> Like it or not, the day came when you bent over, swept up the pieces, glued them together, and took it from there. You yourself were a matter of what you did with the pieces.

> If this was true of me, it was true of my sons as well. If it tore the heart out, the weight of Allen had to be lifted. The sorrow of him and of the harm I'd done him were blocks on the road to usefulness. Lift him up and let him go, *let him go.* Even if he was still alive, I still had to let him go. Allen's outcome was Allen's business. Grief could no longer block me from forgiving myself in order that I might learn to forgive all. "So, son, you are released! My love pries you loose. My love hands you over to Him Who is the Source of comfort."

She closes this experience with a strange statement, filled with keen insight: "I ached with the loss of my grief."

Where love is involved, where loved ones tear at the heart, the prayer of commitment often induces the prayer of relinquishment. It must have been that type of prayer that Abraham prayed as he climbed the mountain with his son and promised heir. It is one of the most difficult prayers we pray: "Lord, here it is; Lord, here he [or she] is; Lord, here I am; You have me." It is the only way into the cycle.

The illustration of a cycle is simply another approach to the words of Jesus in John 15:4, "Abide in me, and I in you. As the branch cannot bear fruit of itself, except it abide in the vine; no more can ye, except ye abide in me." It is a cycle of abiding.

CHAPTER THREE

Trust—Lean Hard

Pastor, I have really committed everything, including myself, to the Lord. Now what do I do?"

"There is only one thing to do—lean hard! You have changed from independence to dependence. You don't just lean; you lean on Someone well able to carry your weight, the One who created the heavens and the earth and who never fails."

The smile of understanding made me realize another one had entered into the cycle.

Trust is a key word in the psalms. It is the word that weaves in and out of the cycle. "Trust in the Lord and do good; inhabit the land and practice faithfulness" (37:3, MEB).

The Amplified Bible translates the word for trust as "lean on, rely on, and be confident." I like to link that definition with the words of David Livingstone, who for the thousandth time placed his finger on the text on which he literally staked his life—"Lo, I am with you always, even unto the end of the world." Then, on the evening of January 14, 1856, he wrote in his diary, "It is the word of a gentleman of the most strict and sacred honour, so there's an end of it!" This immensely lonely man, dying on his knees, left a last entry in his journal, "He will keep His word, the Gracious One, full of grace and truth; no doubt about it. He will keep His word, and it will be all right. Doubt is here inadmissible, surely!" God kept His sacred pledge.

If faith is nothing apart from its object, the same is true of trust, for they are closely akin in meaning. The recommendation from Scripture is to lean hard on the Lord. He made heaven and earth. He calms the storms and stills the waves. His is the earth "and the fullness thereof; the world, and they that dwell therein" (Psalm 24:1). He is the One on whom you lean. All your weight on all of Him! One feels lighter after casting his cares on the Lord. Once you find release through commitment and trust, leaning hard becomes another forward move in the cycle. Here is meaningful, sanctified living, filled with adventure.

Recently I saw an interesting advertisement for a financial concern. They were calling on the public to take a realistic view of making out wills and offering the services of their trust department. Their ad closed with these words: "Trust us. After all, *Trust* is a very important part of our name" (Commerce Bank and Trust Company). Would God not say that to us? "Trust is a very important part of My name."

This call of God requires an active response. We do not place our trust in God and sit back and do nothing. A very important part of this transaction is expressed in the words of Mary: "Whatsoever he saith unto you, do it." The result then was that the water was turned into wine. But the waterpots had to be filled first. The Bible says for us to "trust . . . and do good." Doing good, having an obedient spirit, is an absolute necessity. We are freed from our burden, not to sit down but to run with patience the race set before us. One cannot run entangled in cumbersome cares.

I am sure you realize it is possible anywhere along life's journey for fret to set in. Satan will not cease his efforts to get us out of orbit. He usually attacks the mind and seeks to insert insidious little doubts that, if allowed to, will easily start us toward fret. God's call for us not to fret is not only a requirement for entering the cycle but also a requirement for remaining in it. The opportunity to fret will always present itself; but as trust becomes more and more our way of life, we become less aware of the assaults on our faith.

I remember very vividly how easily I could have slipped out of the cycle of victorious living as I faced a staggering problem in one of my pastorates. First a pall of concern—good, legitimate concern—settled over my spirit. It was not long before I sensed that this concern was becoming seeded with fear. The clouds lowered over my spirit, and I moved into a gray world. In my praying I was telling the Lord everything He already knew. I was actually making my apprehension verbal and getting mighty close to a condition of fret.

After about two days of such suffering, as I was driving to the church one morning, God "climbed" into the car beside me.

"Who asked you to come to this church in the first place?" He asked.

"Why, You did, Lord," I replied.

"Well, then, all you need to do is to obey Me one step at a time. Give Me the problem and do as I say. This church does not belong to you; it belongs to Me!"

I rolled each care over on Him. Thanking Him for His faithful reminder to me that I was getting out of orbit, I found thanksgiving filling my heart.

It was the same process I followed back in 1960 while on that deputation tour. But it was a new situation, so the continuous process went on. Incidentally, need I add, the problem was gloriously taken care of, beyond all I could ask or think. Moffatt translates Psalm 37:5, "Leave all to him, rely on him, and he will see to it." And that is exactly what He did.

There is a little chapel in Basim, India, that has a special significance to me. As resident missionary, I was responsible for the supervision of its construction in 1950, and soon after its completion our youngest son was dedicated at its altar by Dr. C. Warren Jones, at that time the retired foreign missions secretary.

One very hot day I stood at a distance watching the master mason do his work. Each stone was carefully fit into place, and many hands were required to complete the job. About a dozen coolies shuffled past me carrying head loads of crushed rock, which were handed up a shaky scaffold to the mason who properly mixed the cement and worked it around the larger, specially dressed stones. I did not realize the importance of the coolies until the Lord and I had a conversation.

"How closely you watch the master mason!" He said.

"Yes, Lord. He is an artist, and his work is fascinating."

"But you have paid no attention to the coolies shuffling along beside you, have you?"

I was taken aback a bit as I said, "Coolies? Yes, but what they are doing doesn't interest me like the skilled work of the mason."

Then He got all of my attention as the lesson He was teaching me came through: "Son, you are nothing but a coolie in My work. I am the Master Mason. Keep on handing Me what I need, and I will see that the Kingdom is built."

How many times since that hot day have I reminded myself that I am nothing but a coolie; yet there could be no work done in a land like India without them. And again the deep meaning of the phrase in verse 5 burned into my spirit: "Trust . . . and he shall bring it to pass."

Paul expressed the same thought in a familiar scripture: "I planted, Apollos watered, but God [all the while] was making it grow, and [He] gave the increase" (1 Corinthians 3:6, AMP).

CHAPTER FOUR

Delight—Look Up

The clouds hung low that year in India. My wife and infant son were ill, and the heavens were as brass with no apparent penetration. We were pressed beyond measure. One hot, still morning my wife came to me with the baby in her arms and said, "Take care of him for a while; I must find my way through this darkness. I am going to pray and not return until I have found an answer."

Her experience is best expressed in these words she penned afterward:

I closed the door and knelt down by the bed and cried out my heart's agony. "O God, show me the way through, for I have no way to turn!" As I waited, a quiet voice spoke to me; "Look on the table beside the bed. You'll see the answer there."

I was a bit startled but arose and walked over to the little night table. A small book lay on the table and the title, in letters of fire, read "REJOICE." Then God spoke to me again, saying, "Here is the way through; praise Me and delight in Me for myself alone and I will come to your rescue."

It sounds easy when one writes it, but to practice praise under the circumstances took a bit of rethinking. I had been so consumed by the pressures of the problem as well as extreme physical weakness that to be able to express joy seemed an impossibility.

As I knelt again to pray, I was reminded by the Lord of my grandmother. My grandparents gave over

20 years of their lives as missionaries in the north of India. During the latter years of her life my grandmother came to live with my mother. I loved her dearly and enjoyed talking to her about her many experiences as a missionary. She was afflicted with severe attacks of asthma. Many times I heard the sound of her thin little voice in the early morning gasping out between painful wheezings, "Praise the Lord! Hallelujah! Glory to God!"

One morning, as I took her breakfast try to her, I was deeply upset and I asked rather exasperatedly, "Grandma, what do you have to praise the Lord for? Why are you using your strength like this?" To my young mind things did not add up.

She smiled as she looked at me and said, "I praise God for who He is, not for what comes into my life! I guess you would call it the sacrifice of praise. It brings peace to my heart and makes the suffering easier to bear."

Now many years later, far away in a foreign land, the memory returned to me and the great lesson it taught. The sacrifice of praise—how wonderful!

After asking forgiveness, I began to praise the Lord with a heart filled with gratitude for all *He was to me*. Soon the brassy heavens began to melt, a shower of glory fell around my soul, and the clouds of depression and darkness vanished into the sunlight of His presence.

As my wife shared this experience with me, we both turned a corner into a new way of life. It was the way of *purposeful delight.*

The psalmist also reminds us that if we delight in the Lord, we will have the desires of our hearts. What desires? It is rather miraculous how delighting in God purifies these desires! Try it, and you will discover for yourself what I mean.

We find the New Testament equivalent in Philippians 4:4—"Rejoice in the Lord alway: and again I say, Rejoice."

This great truth of delight in the Lord is one that Satan continually tries to blur, and I would want to make it not only brighter in our thinking, but sharper in outline. For I believe here is where we have a deep problem in our cycle. Too often we forget to rejoice in the Lord. It is a matter of remembering to say, "Thank You." It means we revere the Giver more than His gift.

Once again I want to use an acrostic for a definition. To me, delighting in the Lord means—

*D*aily

*E*verything

*L*aid

*I*nto

*G*od's

*H*ands

*T*riumphantly

The matter of delighting daily and *triumphantly* keeps us in the cycle with increased momentum.

When we delight in the Lord, we lift up our eyes with deliberate intent; it is a matter of the will, not the emotions. But it often refreshingly affects the emotions.

Paul tells us to be transformed by the renewing of our minds. Delighting in the Lord is a process; it's a practice and can become a splendid habit. Perhaps some of you are familiar with the painting *The Song of the Lark*. It depicts a young gleaner, standing in the field with upturned face, her monotonous work forgotten for a brief moment as she listens to the musical call of a lark. That's what delighting in the Lord does; it is hearing His call in the midst of life's humdrum and responding with an upturned spirit of praise.

The dimension of delight is actually limitless; like circling ripples in a lake, it reaches to the very shores of heaven. There is a running-over quality about it, an effervescence, a prodigality that spills over into a divine certainty. J. B. Phillips translates Romans 8:38-39, "I have become absolutely convinced that neither death nor life, neither messenger of Heaven nor monarch of earth, neither what happens today nor what may happen tomorrow, neither a power from on high nor a power from below, nor anything else in God's whole world has any power to separate us from the love of God in Jesus Christ our Lord!" What a joyous declaration of faith! *Faith* makes joy possible, not circumstances. The center of our joy is Jesus Christ, the Son of God.

A detour along a highway implies that the regular direct route is closed. Our enemy seeks to place detour signs on the highway of holy living that say, "Take this roundabout way; deviate from the direct path." Detours from delight plunge us into the bumpy side road of fret, and there is nothing to do but to back up, confess our need, and continue on the high road, blessing the Lord at all times, with His Word continually in our mouths.

I like the story of the Israelites given in 2 Chronicles, chapter 20. Singers were appointed who were to praise the Lord in the beauty of holiness. In verse 22 we read, "And when they began to sing and to praise, the LORD set ambushments against the children of Ammon . . . and they were smitten." Jehoshaphat would never have known victory from the enemy apart from these songs of praise. It is *our* best way, also, of overcoming our enemy. Delight is demonstrated in victory. After we cease our fretting, commit our way unto the Lord, and trust in Him, we are able to rejoice in Him who "is the delight of our life as well as the life of our delight."

Delight is contagious. We can be carriers of the delight of the Lord. When I was a boy, our home was stricken with diphtheria, and it was discovered that I was the culprit; I was the carrier of this disease. You know what our world needs? It needs Christians filled with delight exposing people to it wherever they go—in schools and hospitals, at desks, in garages and shops—people contagious for Christ. God wants us to be delightful Christians—delight-filled.

Unfortunately, one cannot get an injection of delight. The villagers in India never felt they had been properly treated by the doctor unless they received an injection. They could be given a handful of pills with explicit directions as to their use, but unless they got an injection they were not satisfied. But God's way is a handful of directives, and unless we follow Him explicitly, there can be no delight. It is through obedience that we discovery joy. I like C. S. Lewis' definition of praise: "Inner health made audible." It is not an isolated experience; it is a way of life.

I find it is best as F. B. Meyer expressed it, to "keep short accounts with God." It is good to have a daily check during our devotions to see if we are delighting in the Lord. No hidden, unclean corners, no sweeping of life under the rug. (Too often this type of a rug gets pulled out from under us! It can be quite embarrassing.) *D*aily *E*verything *L*aid *I*nto *G*od's *H*ands *T*riumphantly—our finances, our mental life, our home life, our business, our friends and associates. Nothing left out.

One translator uses for "delight" the word "relish." It implies something of a distinct flavor that we enjoy eating. What do you suppose David meant when he said, "O taste and see that the Lord is good"? His taste is not bitter and sour but flavorful and sweet.

I wonder what our Master thinks when He looks into our shriveled hearts so lacking in praise and joyousness. It seems that we know everything about life in the Spirit except how to live it! With gracious understanding He would teach us how to live victoriously, that we might bear much fruit.

John Philip Sousa, known as "the march king," was surprised one day to hear floating up into his hotel room the strains of his favorite march, "The Stars and Stripes Forever." It was being played in a slow, lazy, dragging manner by an organ grinder in the street below.

He dashed down into the street. "Here, here!" he called to the sleepy organ grinder. "That is no way to play my march!"

He seized the handle and turned it vigorously. The music came out spirited and happy, and the little organ grinder smiled and bowed low to Mr. Sousa.

The next night Mr. Sousa heard his song again, and this time the tempo was right. He looked out his window and noticed a large sign over the organ with the grinder's name on it and underneath the words, "Pupil of John Philip Sousa."

If we ever learn to delight in the Lord—and we must—we will write under the joys of our lives, "Pupil of Jesus Christ."

What about receiving the desires of our hearts? Strangely enough, before we learn this secret of delight, we are inclined to think of all the things we would like to have; but after delight becomes a way of life, after we learn the secret of victorious living in the Spirit, our lives become uni-directional—we want most of all to be like Him and to live out His love for others. Everything else becomes a happy extra.

CHAPTER FIVE

Rest or Cash In

While my family and I were vacationing in beautiful British Columbia we visited a special farm where Scottie dogs were trained to do all kinds of tricks. They were dressed up in children's clothes, made to jump through hoops, roll barrels, climb ladders, and do numerous things that dogs do not ordinarily do. The trainer always had a pocket filled with tidbits, and for every trick well done the dogs were rewarded with a word of encouragement and a tidbit. It was the old system of reward for disciplined performance. But the reward was never given until after the learning attempt was made.

Perhaps we move here from the ridiculous to the sublime, but there is a related point worthy of consideration. You may well ask me, "Why can't I go from commitment to rest? Why must I go through the full cycle of trust and delight?"

If we do not come the route of trust and delight we are hardly ready for the benefit of rest. Rest is usually hard-earned. The writer to the Hebrews admonishes, "Let us labour therefore to enter into that rest" (Hebrews 4:11). Or as *The Amplified Bible* says, "Let us therefore be zealous and exert ourselves and strive diligently to enter into that rest [of God]." As the man who has come up the hard way in the financial world truly appreciates the value of money, so through obedience to personal disciplines do we know the real meaning of the word *rest*. There are divine patterns that must be followed or we cannot know the joy of "cashing in" on our investment in the Spirit.

This way of life is God's will for every child of His; it is not an option. He has designed a way for us, clear, direct, and attractive. It is to our advantage to follow instructions.

Kierkegaard tells the story of a wild duck who decided to alter his pattern of life. As he was flying south with his fellow ducks, he happened to see on the ground below him some corn a farmer had scattered for his barnyard fowls. So the lazy fellow fluttered down, joined the other ducks, ate the corn, and lingered on. Enjoying the food and security of the barnyard, he forgot about his flying companions and spent the winter in ease.

One spring day he heard the call of the wild ducks overhead as they were flying north. Something deep within him responded to the wild call, and he tried to spread his wings. He fluttered up the best he could, but he had grown fat and flabby and could fly only as far as the eaves of the barn. He watched with despair as his former friends disappeared into the sky, leaving him earthbound to security.

This story is too often a depiction of our lives. We are made for personal victory in Christ Jesus. The plan is clear; the cycle is obvious. Yet we have allowed some deviation to destroy the call of the sky and have succumbed to living in "barnyard security" with wings helpless because of lack of use. This condition is not resting in the Lord; it is a condition of rusting in ourselves.

The rest I speak about is an active rest. He speaks; I listen and obey. And with each new situation I find my way through the cycle to inner rest. It is a rest from friction, not a rest from action. I like the words of Major

Shupp of the Marine Corps, who years ago said, "If we can read it, we can do it." There is a rest in doing when it is in the Lord.

We should be sure to differentiate between *ease* and *rest*. Amos cries out, "Woe to them that are at ease in Zion." Here is a picture of the barnyard duck. There is a great difference between comforts and comfort. People can live in ease but not experience rest. John D. Rockefeller was asked how much money it took to make a man happy. Speaking from experience he said, "Just a little bit more!" The rest God has for us enables us to abound in fruitful and tireless service to Him.

In Psalm 37 David reminds us to "rest in the LORD, and wait patiently for him." The root from the Hebrew is "to cease, to be silent, or submit in silence to what He ordains." God has directives for us which cannot be received clearly until the inner station of the heart is quiet. The still, small voice may have something to say to us that will change our life's direction. We are never too old for this to be a possibility; it keeps a stretch in the soul, the stretch of anticipation.

Because "yes" becomes the language of the heart, we are able to live in relaxed readiness to God's will for our lives. A word of warning might be helpful here. We are talking about a cycle because life actually seems to move in cycles. It seems that we no sooner handle one problem or one situation than another one arises. The relationship is not disturbed because we know we are in Him, but the enemy tries with each new situation to bring in a spirit of fret. Repeatedly we turn from the possibility of fret to *commitment* of the new situation we are facing, *trusting* that He who has helped us thus far will continue to help and *praising* Him for victory. Thus we move back into a state of rest. Perhaps it could be likened to the erratic flight pattern of a bird that flies in and up and around and back again in the process of getting food or protecting its mate or seeking a place to alight and sing. It's the nature of bird life to do this. Nor is our life static. It is ever in motion and thus always open to invasion, suggestion, temptation. But our "flight pattern" can always end in rest! That's the glorious truth as was expressed by Anna L. Waring:

> *My heart is resting, O my God;*
> *I will give thanks and sing.*
> *My heart is at the Secret Source*
> *Of every precious thing.*

It's the secret source to which we continually return and where we continually find rest.

When God gives us a directive, remember that unbelief, or even doubt, can cause fret and get us out of the cycle. Phillips translates Hebrews 4:11, "Let us then be eager to know this rest for ourselves, and let us beware that no one misses it through falling into some kind of unbelief." In verse 12 he says, "For the Word that God speaks is alive and active: it cuts more keenly than any two-edged sword: it strikes through to the place where soul and spirit meet, to the innermost intimacies of a man's being: it exposes the very thoughts and motives of a man's heart." Through relaxed readiness, the *r*'s of rest, comes a persistent spirit of faith. Unbelief keeps us from cashing in on our benefits; it is the great robber of that which God has prepared for us. Unbelief is a blinding sin.

The kind of rest I am writing about is creative rest; it consists of enthusiastic *expectation*. I think the young girl Rhoda, written about in Acts, had this kind of feeling. "Prayer was made without ceasing of the church unto God for him [Peter]," but due to Rhoda's spirit of expectation she was able to hear the knock at the gate. Probably the others were praying so loudly they could not hear the answer. Do we sometimes pray ourselves out of faith? It is quite possible. Although she left Peter standing at the gate without having even seen him, she knew his voice and believed in the answer to their prayers. Because of their incredulity, the disciples did not believe Rhoda, but "she constantly affirmed that it was even so." She knew the rest of faith.

There is another prison story in Matthew's Gospel which gives us a picture of how doubt can rob us of our rest. John the Baptist was imprisoned. Out of his dark, cold cell he sent a question to Jesus, "Are you the one who was to come or are we to look for somebody else?" (Matt. 11:3, Phillips). This was an honest query. John wanted to be sure; he was not experiencing unbelief. How patient Jesus is with our questions! He did not rebuke John but gave this beautiful answer (also from Phillips' translation), "Go and tell John what you see and hear—that blind men are recovering their sight, cripples are walking, lepers being healed, the deaf hearing, the dead being brought back to life and the good news is being given to those in need. *And happy is the man who never loses his faith in me.*" These were not the words of a rebuke, but a loving message to the imprisoned, wondering, tempted John. Jesus does not rebuke honesty; He restores heart and a sense of expectation to such a one.

Rest not only means *readiness* and *expectation,* but also implies a steady *satisfaction.* The work of God's grace in sanctifying the believer has long been described as the establishing grace whereby one is established in

God's rest and is satisfied for life to be this way. Paul was nearing the end of his earthly life and expressed his satisfaction with these words: "But none of these things move me, neither count I my life dear unto myself, so that I might finish my course with joy, and the ministry, which I have received of the Lord Jesus, to testify the gospel of the grace of God" (Acts 20:24). God's rest brings great inner poise.

In 1953 we returned to India for our second term. As I was elected field superintendent upon my return, I faced many important and far-reaching decisions. A month later I was scheduled to conduct the preachers' yearly meeting. It was a major project, and I sincerely wanted God's plan for that gathering.

I set to work in prayer and preparation with true zeal. I had attended a rather large number of preachers' meetings and had a fair idea of what I wanted. But it seemed that every plan or idea turned into sawdust in my hands. I prayed all the more, for time was closing in on me. I needed assurance that His plans were mine. At least that is what I thought; actually I wanted to know that my plans were His.

In the midst of my frustration I gave myself to fasting as well as prayer. I searched God's Word for a special, divine signal or direction. Certainly Paul in Ephesians or Philippians would reveal a green light. But those great letters were like Sahara Deserts to me. After a while my feverishness subsided, and I quieted myself before the Lord. It was obvious that I was in the center and God had to get me out of the way. This took a bit of adjustment, for I did not realize what my problem was.

In a time of quiet meditation, God prompted me to read in Exodus, the area where I was having my regular Scripture reading. It was there in chapter 33 that I found my oasis. Moses was in a comparable situation. He was under the cloudy pillar in the Tabernacle, and all the people were standing in their tent doors waiting for God's Word through him. Moses spoke with great boldness as he prayed, "Shew me now thy way."

The startling answer God gave to Moses was my answer too. All the scaffolding of an intense feeling of personal responsibility went tumbling down as I read, "My presence shall go with thee, and I will give thee rest."

His presence would go with me to the preachers' meeting. What more did I need? As I read the full passage I realized that *presence* and *rest* and *glory* were almost synonymous. My heart was swept with praise and thanksgiving as I placed everything completely into God's hands.

Out of that 1953 preachers' meeting came a glory of revival such as I have never experienced before or since. God's rest leads us to *triumph,* the *t* of the acrostic.

And there we have our definition for rest:

*R*eadiness

*E*xpectation

*S*atisfaction

*T*riumph

I want to close this chapter with a meaningful paraphrase of the twenty-third psalm, published in *Guideposts.* It was entitled "23rd PSALM FOR BUSY PEOPLE."

The Lord is my Pacesetter; I shall not rush.

He makes me stop and rest for quiet intervals.

He provides me with images of stillness, which restore my serenity.

He leads me in ways of efficiency, through calmness of mind,

And His guidance is peace.

Even though I have a great many things to accomplish each day

I will not fret, for His presence is here.

His timelessness, His all-importance, will keep me in balance.

He prepares refreshment and renewal in the midst of my activity

By anointing my mind with His oils of tranquility.

My cup of joyous energy overflows.

Surely harmony and effectiveness shall be the fruits of my hours,

For I shall walk in the pace of my Lord, and dwell in His house forever.

—TOKI MIYASHINA

CHAPTER SIX

Jesus Is Lord

During the wonderful outpouring of the Holy Spirit in revival in India in 1954, my wife and I were asked to share our experiences with another denomination in the north of India. We were invited to a well-known hospital compound in Vrindaban, a city where there are as many idols as people. From the very first meeting, the winds of the Spirit began to blow. People were gripped by a spirit of openness and honesty, and prayers of many years were answered.

One afternoon I sat in the old mission bungalow with a fine Indian Christian, a converted Hindu and a Sanskrit scholar. There was an air of brooding about him as he rocked back and forth in a hand-carved rocker. The more we discussed things of the Spirit, the more I sensed his deep dissatisfaction. He had come with a need.

After a few minutes he leaned forward and looked at me intently.

"Mr. Lee," he said, "I want you to tell me what total freedom means. I don't want your answer today; I want you to think about it and to pray about it. But God has told me that you can give me the answer I need."

I was quite astonished. I promised him I would certainly pray about it and mind the Spirit. I went to our room feeling mystified and a bit troubled. What could I tell this great scholar? But I quickly realized it would not be I; it would be Christ.

Two days later we returned to the historic old parlor in which he had found Christ years before. (He was converted through reading the Bible.) With a look of anticipation, he sat down in the same old rocking chair.

I waited a bit before speaking. Finally I said, "The answer seems so simple I am hesitant to give it; yet I feel it is from the Lord."

"I know it is from the Lord," he promptly replied. "Let's hear it. I'm ready."

"Well, it's simply this: If the Son makes you free, you are free indeed, and that means *freedom* in *things, not freedom* from *things.*"

He closed his eyes, leaned back in his chair for a few seconds, then said, "Say that again."

"God wants to free you where you are, not take you out of the situation," I replied.

"Say it once again."

I repeated the thought.

With tears filling his dark brown eyes, he reached over and placed my big hand in his strong brown hands and said, "I accept it. That's the truth I need: freedom *in* things, not freedom *from* things. Thank you."

He arose from the chair and with a look of peace said, "I'll do it. I'll accept what must be accepted and find my freedom right where I am." He walked from the room with determination.

He said nothing more to me at the time, and I left the room thoroughly mystified. Later on I discovered how beautifully the Holy Spirit had guided. This man was embroiled in a delicate and difficult family situation from which there was no escape. God showed him that the escape was within himself, in his attitude toward the situation. Through a marvelous series of events, God worked things out beyond our asking or thinking.

The entire week was a week of miracles. When it came time to leave, Mr. C— rode with me in a horse-drawn tonga to the station. We shared the rich experiences of the week. Our fellowship in Christ was very warm. The train was approaching the station, and we were in the process of giving luggage to the coolies when he turned to me rather abruptly and said, "Do you know what 'Jesus is Lord' really means?"

Sensing he wanted a negative answer, I told him I did not know.

"Well, 'Jesus is Lord' means He is my Owner; He is my Possessor," and with a hearty slap on my shoulder he added, "He is my Dispossessor!"

As he spoke, the train roared in, coolies grabbed the luggage, and I had very little time to reply. I thanked him warmly, and we waved good-bye.

Later in the night I thought about what he had said to me. "Jesus is Lord" is a phrase E. Stanley Jones uses over and over again with three fingers held high. Mr. C— was giving names to those three fingers: Owner . . . Possessor . . . Dispossessor. I recalled the words of Job: "The LORD gave, and the LORD hath taken away; blessed be the name of the LORD" (1:21 emphasis added).

Job's testimony came after he had lost everything dear to him. He suffered bereavement and questions and misunderstanding and bodily pain. But he blessed the name of the Lord, who, though He had dispossessed him of all he had, had not disinherited him. The thing that mattered most remained—his relationship with his God.

I wondered what God had removed from this Indian scholar to make him free. I never actually knew, but later he wrote a postscript to his well-known autobiography telling about his newfound freedom in the Spirit. That was answer enough!

Jesus is Lord is the great center of the cycle of victorious living. The key phrase from each of these four verses in Psalm 37 is *"in the LORD."* "Commit thy way *unto the LORD*"; "Trust *in the LORD*"; Delight . . . *in the LORD*"; "Rest *in the LORD.*" This kind of living demands a sacramental view of life where everything is done unto the Lord. All our being as well as our doing must answer the question: "Is Jesus Christ the Center?" Not that we might feel better, or work more effectively, but that in all things He might have the glory.

E. Stanley Jones says that either Jesus is Lord *of all* or He is not Lord *at all.* Too often we give the testimony, "Jesus means everything to me," when all the time someone else or something else is at the center of our lives. The center must be right, or everything else is off balance. If we miss this truth we miss everything. No matter how good our center may be, *if it is other than Jesus Christ,* it is not good enough. Remember—our center controls us, as the hub controls the wheel. He is "the summing up of all that man needs."

Jesus is Lord was the creed of the Early Church, and since the Resurrection it is the great recurring theme in the symphony of the kingdom of God.

The generation of today asks, What difference does it make? What difference does it make that Jesus is Lord?

If Jesus is Lord, life has meaning. He makes the difference between victory and defeat, between hope and despair, between life and death.

Too many circles of philosophical thought end in a "horror of darkness." Inability to communicate is one of the great problems of existentialism. Like a figure in a nightmare, man wants to cry out, but he has no voice. Jesus Christ gives us a voice, a purpose, a center by *being* the Voice, the Purpose, the Center. He makes all the difference in the world.

The rich young man, pressed in by life, came running up to Jesus to ask, "Good Master, what shall I do that I may inherit eternal life?" He was sincere; he was troubled; he really wanted an answer.

Jesus loved him as He looked on him and longed for him to fulfill his personhood. But the young man lacked one thing, allegiance to Christ, which would mean cutting off from all his earthly supports. Christ placed His finger on the vulnerable spot as He said, "Go . . . sell . . . give . . . and come, take up the cross, and follow me" (Mark 10:21). The young man turned away, sorrowful. His center controlled him, and his center was self. The words of Christ were action words, words demanding a reversal of direction. They were words that spelled a cross.

If we were to draw a line vertically and one horizontally through the center of our diagram, we would form a cross. At that point we find Jesus Christ. Everything we *commit* is committed to the Cross; our *trust* is wholly in the Cross; our *delight* is in the Cross, as Paul said in Galatians 6:14—"But God forbid that I should glory, save in the cross of our Lord Jesus Christ, by whom the world is crucified unto me, and I unto the world." And our *rest,* too, is in the finished work of Christ on the Cross, for "every day we experience something of the death of Jesus, so that we may also know the power of the life of Jesus in these bodies of ours."

It is through Him that we live and move and *have our being*. He gets into our personalities, our hang-ups, our subconscious, needy selves and creates a growing edge that continues until life is over. We are ever discovering our potential in Him and moving in a "divine crescendo" more and more to the perfect day. He heals wounds and is continually helping us with our infirmities, our complexes, our "maladjustive impulses," our "damaged emotions." Romans 8:11 says, "Once the Spirit of him who raised Jesus from the dead lives within you he will, by that same Spirit, bring to your whole being new strength and vitality" (PHILLIPS). The Holy Spirit is the greatest creative force in the world.

He guides us in our interpersonal relationships. When Jesus is Lord, He controls our friendships, our attitudes, our activities. Peter was quite disturbed about John. Perhaps he was smarting a bit after his soul-searching on the beach. However, he said to Christ, "Lord, and what shall this man do?" Phillips translates Christ's answer, "If it is my wish for him to stay until I come, is that your business, Peter? You must follow me." That puts an end to many unsettling matters. "You must follow me." Any attitude, any liaison, any transaction that keeps us from following Christ is "out of bounds" to us. *Jesus is Lord* leads through a narrow path to life eternal. There is no room for a great deal of impediments.

Who knows better than the Holy Spirit how infirm we are? It is our handful of dust with which He is constantly at work! J. B. Phillips translates 2 Corinthians 4:7, 5, "This priceless treasure we hold, so to speak, in a common earthenware jar—to show that the splendid power of it belongs to God and not to us. . . . For it is Christ Jesus as Lord whom we preach, not ourselves."

In an age of humanism, the Spirit would teach us that He is Host of this universe and we are His guests. But He allows us to "carry around" this great treasure in our homely selves, that we might ever be reminded of our dependence on our God.

What difference does it make? Listen to these words further on: "We are handicapped on all sides, but we are never frustrated; we are puzzled, but never in despair. We are persecuted, but we never have to stand it alone: we may be knocked down but we are never knocked out!" He gives us the ability to keep on going in His power.

I well remember an experience I had several years ago. I sat down to an evening meal with my family as though it were a parenthesis to more important things. During the meal I was somewhat preoccupied. All of a sudden my younger son said, "Dad, do you really have to go out again tonight?"

His question cut into my thinking like a knife. No, I really did not *have* to go calling that night. I decided right then that the most important thing for me that evening was to remain at home with my family. It was a great relief to quit spinning my wheels, have a relaxed spirit, and enjoy the ones I love. The Kingdom would go on, for *Jesus* is Lord, not I!

The cycle of victorious living requires a teachable spirit. In this way we cultivate a heart "at leisure from itself"; we have an inner poise and security from which we fulfill Christ's command to *go*, to *tell*, to *do*.

When Jesus is Lord we know the deep meaning of the hymn:

> *In service which Thy love appoints*
> *There are no bonds for me;*
> *My secret heart is taught the truth*

That makes Thy children free;
A life of self-renouncing love
Is one of liberty.

—A. L. WARING

So now we move on, and the adventure of life in the cycle never ends. There will be new insights, new joys, new discoveries; for really this total concept is only my way of describing our walk with Jesus Christ. It is life on tip-toes of excitement in the Spirit.

May I say to you, "Have a great time in *your* adventure IN Christ in *the cycle of victorious living.*" Someday we shall talk it over together with our wonderful Lord, who is the center of everything; for "he is before all things, and by him all things consist. And he is the head of the body, the church: who is the beginning, the firstborn from the dead; that in all things he might have the preeminence. For it pleased the Father that in him should all fullness dwell" (Colossians 1:17-19).

Jesus is Lord!

CHAPTER SEVEN

It Works

What father has not sat down with his son with a new toy that needs assembling and said, "Now, let's see. If we follow these directions, I'm sure we'll find out how it works"? Then painstakingly he reads the directions, allowing the boy to do as much of the work as he can. After a time of patience and cooperation, they go outdoors and fly the kite or float the boat or watch the airplane zoom into loops around the backyard. Then the little fellow cries excitedly, "Boy, Dad, we really made it work!"

I would be wasting your time and mine if I were advocating a way of life that did not work. In this book I have tried to give a set of instructions as guidelines to victorious living. I have probably used a new avenue of approach, but it is the same grand, old truth. The testimony of scores of individuals has convinced me it works; it opens the way to a new level of sanctified living.

There are many ways a minister earns his right to share in the lives of his people. Quite often an illuminating truth from the pulpit becomes a passport to a new area of Christian life. Such is this message on the cycle of victorious living, which, because of the response, I preach once a year in my present pulpit.

In a former pastorate was a little lady in the congregation who came faithfully on Sunday mornings but because of ill health was unable to attend other services. She had been widowed for a number of years. While her husband was alive he had almost wrapped her in tissue paper as he tenderly cared for her every need. After his death she had kept going, but on a very slight margin.

She supplied our home with her special brand of jams and jellies. Not long after I had preached my sermon on the cycle of victorious living, I decided our jam supply was low, so I stopped by her home one warm spring day. As I stepped up to her porch I could hardly believe my ears. She was playing the piano and singing a hymn with great gusto. I knocked lightly, as I did not want to disturb her; yet I was extremely curious as to this joyful sound coming from her usually silent house.

I waited until she had finished a verse and then knocked louder. She came to the door with the glow of the music still on her face.

"Why, Sister—," I said in amazement, "I did not know you could sing and play so well. I really enjoyed that!"

"Come in, Pastor, and I'll tell you what has happened to me," she replied as she swung open the door.

I walked into her humble little home and sat near the piano as she shared her experience with me.

"After you preached your sermon on 'the cycle,' I knew there was something in that sermon for me. Since my husband died I have gone on living, but more as an existence. New truth has come through to me, and now I'm really *alive!*

She whirled around on the piano stool, and we sang a duet of joy together. Oh, yes, I got my jars of jelly, but no gift was so great as this heartwarming testimony.

Her health did not improve appreciably. In fact, in a subsequent examination her doctor told her he could not see what was keeping her alive. But she confided in me that everything was committed to the Lord, that she was delighting in "the cycle" and that was reason enough to live.

Since writing of this experience I have received a note from this woman in which she said in part,

> The messages you gave, Brother Lee, on the thirty-seventh psalm still linger with me. Today is the second time I have been out to church since Christmas, but through all the pain and suffering the blessed words linger with me: "Heaven will be worth it all . . ."

Once the truth of this cycle becomes a way of life, it goes on and on through the years, come what may.

Ministers, like doctors, hear from parishioners or patients at odd times and in unexpected places. Mrs. Lee and I had been asked to speak at a Valentine banquet in a neighboring church. It was enjoyable sharing our thoughts with young people—thoughts on love and marriage and compatibility. After the banquet a young woman came up to me and said, "Let me tell you, Brother Lee—that cycle of victorious living really works!"

I was a bit startled to hear this enthusiastic testimony in this port city where I thought I knew no one. "Now where did you hear that?" I asked, quite puzzled.

She opened her Bible where she had especially marked Psalm 37 and reminded me of an indoor camp meeting held in Norwalk, California, where I was the speaker.

"You pulled out a large blackboard and drew the cycle on it and then proceeded to tell us how to live victoriously. I made up my mind that I had better get started in the cycle. That was six months ago, and my life has been completely changed ever since!"

The best part of that banquet for me was to see this woman's radiant face and to share in her joy as she reached a new level of Spirit-filled living.

A friend and I had spent many hours together as we prayed and believed for his spiritual release. The cycle had been a prominent part of our times of sharing. Through God's Word and especially through Psalm 37, he had found many answers for his badly shattered life.

In trying to find his way, he had wisely sought professional help.

One day during our regular visits he surprised me with an account of his most recent session with his doctor. "Believe it or not, Pastor, I took along this little diagram of the cycle and showed it to my doctor."

I was surprised, naturally. Most patients would not have this much courage! "What did he think?" I asked.

"The doctor looked at the cycle as I explained it to him and what it had done for me, and he said, 'This truth is psychologically sound and seems to be a great answer.'

"Then I smiled as I quietly told him the whole principle was found in the Bible, in the thirty-seventh psalm!"

I walked into a hospital room where a teenager was lying flat on her back with a broken leg hoisted up in a splint. An arm also was broken, and her head was severely lacerated. I prayed a prayer of thanksgiving that this young lady was alive, as the car in which she had been riding had been hit by a train and the young driver had been killed. She was a new convert and radiant in her newfound faith.

Several days later I returned to see her and several of her church friends were in the room with her. I walked over to her bed to pray with her, and as I turned, my attention was drawn to something hung above her door. There, staring her right in the face, was the diagram of the cycle of victorious living, which one of her friends had drawn for her.

"Linda," they had said to her, "this is what you need more than anything else right now!"

And with youthful candor she admitted it was true as she added, "Pastor, it has lifted my spirits totally and taken my mind off myself. It is the best prescription of all!"

In order to keep in touch with people in my congregation I have designed a *Friendship in Worship* card. One of the request categories on it states, *Appointment with the Pastor.* One Monday as I was going over these cards, I noticed a young veteran of the Vietnam War had checked the box for an appointment.

Later that week he sat across my desk from me, completely weighed down with burdens of home and family and adjustments that only war veterans would understand. I let him fully unload and then asked him if he was familiar with the cycle of victorious living. As it was new to him, I took out a small card on which the diagram was printed and shared it with him. Then I said, "Have you been filled with the Holy Spirit?"

He was silent for a few seconds. He had been brought up in the church and was almost delighting in some of his "hang-ups." He had learned a commanded discipline in the army, but when on his own, spiritually he found himself extremely undisciplined.

"No, Pastor, I don't believe I have ever asked the Holy Spirit to take over the center of my life. I have been the center," he said quite candidly.

We looked over the cycle again, and I showed him what it meant for Jesus Christ to be Lord of one's life. Self had to be crucified in order for Christ to be Lord. A deliberate transaction was necessary.

Light came to him. He accepted it and prayed a prayer of surrender to the Holy Spirit, confessing his need. Of course, the Holy Spirit came, and the man left my office delighting in the Lord.

A few days later I met him again after the close of a service. He gripped my hand warmly as he said, "Pastor, it works!" I will soon be performing his marriage ceremony, and what a different start his new life will have as he lives in the cycle of victorious living!

Not too long ago I was invited to lunch with a fine member of my church who wished to discuss a means of outreach in his community. It was a stimulating time for both of us.

On our way home I asked him about an automobile accident that he had been involved in the week before. His brand-new car had been demolished. It was a miracle the man was alive.

"Were you wearing your seat belt?" I asked.

"I sure was!" he answered. "But let me tell you how that cycle of victorious living you preach about helped me in that nearly fatal accident. After the impact, I skidded across the intersection, and as I came to a stop I realized I was apparently not seriously injured, but my shiny new car was a wreck. In those first stunned seconds I found myself committing the entire situation to the Lord with a calmness that could come only from the Divine.

"In fact, I was so calm I was able to help the other man involved make out his report. He was greatly upset and nervous.

"The next day I called at his home to see how he was and helped him with more paperwork. He looked at me in amazement as he asked, 'Why are you doing this for me? You have every reason to be doing just the opposite!'

"Then in a flash came the opportunity to explain to this man what Jesus Christ and His peace meant to me. And, Pastor," he added, "the cycle was there in my mind the moment I needed it, and I never had a fretful minute during that entire experience!"

Perhaps this is what Will Huff meant when he talked about "nick-of-time grace." Anyway, it works!

The last example I want to share with you concerns a man I have never met. The fact is, he lived six hundred years before Christ was born. His name was Habakkuk. He looked about and saw the oppression of his people; he looked up and saw the inscrutability of his God; he looked within and saw a living faith. Like David, his faith was his hope in this evil world.

The last three verses of Habakkuk's little book contain some of the most magnificent, imaginative poetry in literature. They also constitute one of the strongest declarations of faith ever written—a moving testimony of the cycle of victorious living:

Although the fig tree shall not blossom,
>*neither shall fruit be in the vines;*
>*the labour of the olive shall fail,*
>*and the fields shall yield no meat;*
>*the flock shall be cut off from the fold,*
>*and there shall be no herd in the stalls:*
Yet I will rejoice in the LORD,
>*I will joy in the God of my salvation.*
The LORD *God is my strength,*
and he will make my feet like hinds' feet,
and he will make me to walk upon mine high places.

The Lord God not only gives strength; He *is* strength. As we *commit, trust, delight,* and *rest* in the Lord, we are enabled to leap up into the heights of God's grace and love, sharing in the heavenly places with our Lord Jesus Christ, "far above all principality, and power, and might, and dominion, and every name that is named, not only in this world, but also in that which is to come" (Ephesians 1:21).